GARDENING NOTES FOR SOUTH CAROLINA

A Garden Book for Zone 7-B, 8-A

2ND EDITION

The Columbia Garden Club

The University of South Carolina Press

© 2005 The Columbia Garden Club

Original paperback edition published by the Columbia Garden Club, 2005
This paperback edition published in Columbia, South Carolina,
by the University of South Carolina Press, 2012

www.sc.edu/uscpress

Manufactured in the United States of America

21 20 19 18 17 16 15 14 13 12   10 9 8 7 6 5 4 3 2 1

ISBN 978-1-57003-850-1 (pbk)

The object of the Columbia Garden Club shall be to promote the love of gardening among amateurs, to protect and promote the growth of our native trees, flowers and birds, and to encourage civic planting and civic beauty.

The Columbia Garden Club Constitution

No occupation is as delightful to me
as the culture of the earth
and no culture comparable
to that of the garden.
Such a variety of subjects,
some one always coming to perfection,
the failure of one thing repaired
by the success of another,
and instead of one harvest
a continued one through the year.

Thomas Jefferson

Table of Contents

INTRODUCTION 4
History of The Columbia Garden Club 6
IMPORTANT SOIL AND PLANTING BASICS 8
Compost 9
Hardiness Zones 9
How to take a Soil Sample 10
Fertilizer labels & pH scale 11
Frost dates 12
Mulch with newspapers 12
Planting tips 13
Pruning tips 14

Gardening by the Month:
WINTER
December 16
Poinsettias 18
Gardening gifts 19
January 20
February 21

SPRING
March 26
Sowing seeds & rooting geraniums 29
April 30
Tomatoe Tips 35
May 36
Lawns 41

SUMMER
June 42
July 44
August 47

FALL
September 49
October 51
November 53
Forcing Paperwhites 57

PERENNIALS 58
Iris, Black eyed Susan, Carolina Jessamine 59
Chrysanthemum 60
Hosta, Angel's Trumpet 61
Ferns 62
Ornamental grasses 63

Day Lily 64
Perennials lists 64
Tropicals 66
ANNUALS 68
Annual lists 70
Endangered Plants list 72
Arbor Day 73
TREES 74
Citrus Trees 75
Palms 78
Shrubs 80
Hydrangeas 82
Camellias 86
Roses 90
LAWNS 96
HERBS 98
EDIBLE FLOWERS 102
BULBS 104
HEIRLOOM PLANTS 108
CONTAINER GARDENING 110
House Plants 114
Coastal Gardening 115
BIRDS 116
Hummingbirds 118
Discouraging deer 120
Carolina Fence Garden 122
Backyard habitat application 124
"Kinder" gardening 126
Water gardening 128
Garden & landscape design 129
Decorating your mansion 130
Lyme Disease 132
Hints for flower arrangement design 134
Conditioning flowers & foliage 139
Fire ant management 144
REFERENCES
Book list 146
Extension Service numbers 148
Catalogs & web sites 149
Gardens to visit 150

Introduction

Gardening is an old South Carolina hobby. Our forefathers found many beautiful native plants in our paradise stretched between the Blue Ridge Mountains and the Atlantic Ocean. The Columbia Garden Club has been shoveling midlands South Carolina dirt for 75 years. We may not all have perfect gardens, but we have been rewarded with hours of learning and great friendships.

A garden club is a wonderful way to share with others the love of gardening. If you are interested in joining a garden club, email The Garden Club of South Carolina at www.gardenclubsc.org or National Garden Clubs, Inc. at www.gardenclub.org.

Gardening here is truly a year-round hobby. We can have blooms all year. We are blessed to have four real weather seasons in the Midlands. Such a blessing is not without its drawbacks: it can feel that we have all four seasons in a single week, and we have more than our share of bugs and dry, hot summers.

Our goal for this collection of notes is to have relevant information for the beginner to intermediate gardener in zones 7-b,8-a. We have also included some of our favorite sources for further study.

These notes are from our collective files. Some were diligently researched and some were from our speakers, which we scribbled on old newspapers complete with coffee and compost stains.

We acknowledge some conflicting information, but that is a part of gardening. Take it as a challenge when an expert says a beautiful plant can not be grown here.

Thank you to all who helped make this notebook possible,

Elizabeth Wyman Crews
Editor

Contributing Columbia Garden Club Members:

Verd Cunningham	Ginger Blencowe	Joanne Campbell
Nell Brennen	Patsy Black	Paulette Freeman
Mary Lewis	Ann Smith	Andrella Brunson
English Folsom	Elizabeth Richards	Beth Kibler
Nica Sweeny	Ginny Meynard	Sharon Vanzant
Carol Popp	Jane Suggs	Margaret Wyman
Amy Dawson	Sally McWilliams	Ellen Westfall
Susan DePass	Cricket Newman	Caroline Matthews
Lucy Eggleston	Becky Austin	Christy Snipes Bowers
Bibs Hurt	Susie Heyward	Suzanne Porter
Meekin Herlong	Marshall Foster	Debra Paysinger
Carol Black	Evie Bunge	Emily Tompkins
Janet Cotter	Sally Ames	Jimmilib Harrison
Yvonne Russell	Chris Myers	Nancy Theus
Emily Lumpkin	Julia Keenan	Meg Fant
Connie Smith	Mary Mac Cain	
Betty Maseng	Betsy Daniel	

...And the entire membership of The Columbia Garden Club

Members of the Community:

Leif E. Maseng
Sam F. Crews

Life begins the day you start a garden.

— Chinese Proverb

History of the Columbia Garden Club

Founded in 1926 with 73 members, the Columbia Garden Club has promoted a love of gardening among amateurs, protected our native trees, flowers, and birds through conservation, and encouraged civic beautification by sponsoring plantings in both public and private places.

Among the many contributions to our community by the club are the biannual plant exchange. We have also helped support the beautification of the Wales Garden Parkway, Township Auditorium, Senate Street Parkway, Saluda Avenue, chapel at Fort Jackson, County Alms House, and park at Laurel and Lincoln Streets. We also helped on Highway 215, at the mini-park at Harden and Heyward Streets, at Five Points, on Elmwood Ave., and landscaped the Teardrop Garden at Richland Memorial Hospital. We continue to plant roses in honor of our deceased members at our own Memorial Rose Garden on the Horseshoe at the University of S.C.

The club donated hundreds of plants to the church garden of Bethel African Methodist Episcopal Church, and has donated time and money to the Robert Mills House, Columbia Green, Boylston Gardens, and Hampton-Preston House.

The Columbia Garden Club Foundation was established in 1983. Its initial funding was generated by the sale of property donated to the Columbia Garden Club in 1950 by Miss Janie Dent. With income from investments and proceeds from the club's house tours, early contributions to the community by the Foundation have included funds for the Woodrow Wilson Boyhood Home, S.C. State Museum, Babcock Center, Riverbanks Zoo, Columbia Museum of Art, Sidney Park, Arbor Day, Richland County Public Library, and Columbia Green.

Recent Foundation projects include funds for expansion of the Memorial Rose Garden at the University of S.C., Botanical Garden at Clemson University, Capital Senior Center, Botanical Garden at Riverbanks Zoo,

Columbia Museum of Art, Palmetto Greenway Initiative, the landscaping at Carolina Children's Home with club members participating in the work, and annual scholarships in support of conservation efforts. As of May 1999, the Foundation had dispersed over $140,000 towards these projects.

Other community projects requiring the time and talents of club members include decorating the Governor's Mansion for Christmas (since 1981), and making flower arrangements for special events at the University of S.C., S.C. State Museum, Columbia Museum of Art, and S. C. Archives and History Foundation. A special project of the club is the Annual Clara Albergotti Memorial Standard Flower Show.

Many local and national awards have been presented to the Columbia Garden Club throughout the years for its work in conservation and civic beautification.

The first woman horticulturist in America to be published, was from the Province of South Carolina. In 1752, Mrs. Martha Daniell Logan wrote a "Gardener's Kalendar." She was remembered as a lady, and "esteemed a very good one."

Important Soil and Planting Basics

TYPES OF SOIL

Sandy soil usually is well-drained (often too dry) requiring clay and other amendments to be added to hold water. But as the water easily drains through sand, so do nutrients. Some amendments to try to hold nutrients are mushroom compost and peat moss. Compost provides nutrients and retains water, while peat moss just retains water. In most cases, mushroom compost will do the trick.

Clay soil drains poorly but does store nutrients. Clay sticks together when wet and bonds like a brick when it dries. Add sand to promote better drainage and help air reach the plant roots. The Clemson University Extension Service recommends mixing in gypsum to break up the clay. There are no definitive guidelines regarding the application rate of gypsum for gardeners. It is sparingly soluble and thus it is nearly impossible to apply too much. Generally, a gardener should just sprinkle a fine layer over the soil surface and work it in.

Loam is a mixture of sand and clay. This is the best general soil for growing plants. Loam is the kind of soil found on the forest floor or along a river basin. It's loaded with decayed plant material, which translates to organic nutrients for plants. The perfect flower bed or vegetable garden consists of 50 percent soil, 5 percent organic matter, and the rest air and water.

Drainage is important. Perform this easy exercise to test the drainage in your garden: Dig a hole about the size of a small shrub transplant and fill it with water. If there is water still in the hole after 24 hours, your soil drains poorly and will need amendments to correct it.

Before everything else, getting ready is the secret of success.
— Henry Ford

A compost pile is a wonderful source of organic matter, but it must be maintained or it can breed flies and smell bad. Generally it is a pile of debris which is layered with soil, watered and turned regularly. You may add leaves, lawn clippings, raw kitchen wastes, coffee grounds, dust & lint, and even well soaked newspapers. But be careful what you add to it. Avoid cooked food scraps, and anything with grease, as well as diseased plants, the roots of perennial weeds and the seeds of annual weeds. Worms are the workers in the pile and must be encouraged. But worms do not like onions. They will actually crawl out of the heap if it has onions or other intensely acidic food particles in it.

Sludge is a good thing. The East Richland County Public Service District has an answer for gardeners with "tired soil." It is selling sludge, a rich compost, although pungent, to the public. The material increases the water holding capacity of sandy soils and adds needed organic material to heavy clay. Call 788-6351 for information or call your county extention service.

USDA Hardiness Zone Map for South Carolina:

Small tip of north-west mountains is 7-A.
Generally from Columbia towards the north-west is 7-B.
Generally from Columbia towards the south-east is 8-A.
Narrow coastal strip is 8-B.

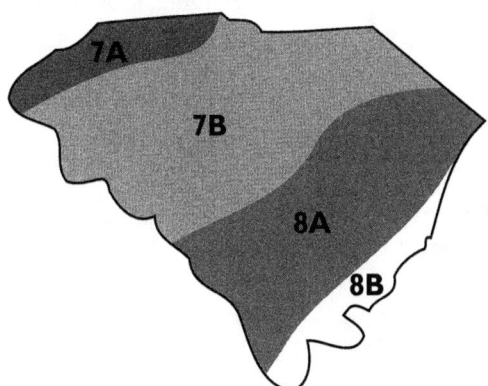

We are considered by most as the Middle South.
Southern Living considers us Lower South.

HOW TO TAKE A SOIL SAMPLE

Soil is the basis of everything in the garden, and if you have healthy soil, gardening will be easy. To start a garden you need to find out the status of your soil. A general soil test will inform you of the Ph and specific fertilizer needs of your soil. You may also request particular tests like organic matter, nitrogen and salt (which coastal gardeners should get).

To have a soil sample analyzed, take different samples from unrelated areas (for instance, the front and back yard) or areas that have received very different treatment (for instance, the lawn and vegetable garden). Depending on the size of the area to be tested, choose 6-18 different spots from which to take soil. In the case of grass, you will want to test the top 4". All other tests should go to a depth of 6-8".

At each spot, dig a funnel-shape hole to the required depth and set the soil aside. Then scrape the edges of the hole for the dirt to be used in your sample— that way, you will have an even top-to-bottom mix. Or you can use a corer to plunge straight down and use the soil it brings up. Mix the soil from all 6-18 spots together very well, making sure you have three (3) cups of soil in the sample.

Do not take the sample when your soil is wet, as it cannot be sent away until it is dry. If you are taking more than one sample, be sure to make a note for yourself explaining which is Sample #1, etc. Your report will refer only to the sample number. You will receive a computer printout by mail in 2-3 weeks.

Cost per sample is $6.00

Richland County ....(803) 865-1216
900 Clemson Road, Columbia, S.C.

Lexington County ....(803) 359-8515
605 West Main Street, Lexington, S.C.

Or take to
Woodley's Garden Center ....(803) 788-1487
10015 Two Notch Road, Columbia, S.C.

Understanding Fertilizer Labels

All fertilizers are labeled with three numbers.

The first number is always **nitrogen**. It is generally for above ground growth: i.e., luxuriant stem and green foliage (Leaves). Deficiency is shown by slow growth and yellowing. Nitrogen leaches readily from soil, especially during periods of high rainfall. Fertilizers with high first numbers (like 31-3-7) are used mostly for lawns.

The second number is always **phosphorus**. This mineral ripens tissues, promotes strong root systems, incrreases fruits and blooms (flowers). Deficiency is shown by poor growth and dull reddish-purple leaves. Fertilizers with high second numbers (like 11-40-6, "Bloom-Busters") increase flowering of annuals and perennials.

The third number is always **potassium**, which builds disease resistance, strong roots and bulbs (roots). Deficiency is shown by scorch around leaf edge which moves inward between veins. It leaches readily from soil, especially during periods of high rainfall. Fertilizers with high third numbers (like 8-8-25) are used mostly for winterizing warm season grasses to aid vigor and winter hardiness.

For fertilizer, remember in this order:
Leaves, Flowers, Roots

---

pH is the symbol indicating the acidity – alkalinity scale: Have a soil sample analyzed to determine yours. Raise the pH with dolomitic limestone. Lower it with sulfur. Lime improves overly-acidic soil. But have patience. It takes several months to change the pH of your soil.

The scale is from 0 to 14:
4.5 very acid, 7 is neutral, 9.1 is very alkaline.

❄ AVERAGE FROSTS

CITY	FIRST	LAST
Greenville	October 8	May 5
Conway	October 26	April 3
Columbia	October 16	April 17
Beaufort	November 1	March 28

MULCH WITH NEWSPAPERS

Make good soil into great healthy soil that doesn't have weeds and doesn't need fertilizer. Patricia Lanza has written three books about what she calls "lasagna." It is easy: for the first layer spread something heavy to smother existing grass and weeds. Do not use black plastic because it causes too much heat to build up, killing earth worms, which are the real workers in this garden. Overlap thick pads of newspaper or cardboard, then wet it. Next add a 2 to 3 inch layer of peat moss. Next add a 4 to 8 inch layer of organic mulch, which can be commercially bought or made up of shredded leaves, animal manure, compost, grass clippings, vegetable peels and coffee grounds. Then add another layer of peat moss followed by a layer of mulch until the bed is 18 to 24 inches deep. You can also add bone meal or wood ash on the top. Pull apart the layers to make holes for setting plants into, then pull the mulch back around the plants and water thoroughly.

Gardening is ... an outlet for fanaticism, violence, love and rationality without their worst side.

— Geoffrey Charlesworth

The kiss of the sun for pardon,
The song of the birds for mirth,
One is nearer God's Heart in a garden
Than anywhere else on earth.

— Dorothy Frances Gurney

PLANTING TIPS:

Organic matter helps all kinds of soil. Good sources of organic matter are sphagnum peat moss, ground pine bark, well-rotted animal manure (never raw manure), decomposed leaves & decomposed grass clippings (unless lawn was treated with herbicide). Your own compost pile is wonderful, (remember – no onions) and do not use sawdust as a mulch. When adding organic matter to your garden, always include the original soil, so that the roots will not stop when they get to the edge of the prepared hole. A good site to find all about organic gardening is www.gardensalive.com.

There are two different ideas when it comes to planting. The one I'm sure you've heard is "plant a $1.00 plant in a $10.00 hole." Some research, however, seems to indicate that water and nutrients have difficulty passing between enriched and ordinary soil, and that roots may actually slow (or go around) when they hit a barrier of unfamiliar soil. So, be careful to mix some enriched soil with the surrounding dirt.

The size of the hole does matter. Generally dig the hole twice as wide as the plant, but be very careful that you do not plant it too deep. Plant at the same level as the plant was in the nursery pot, as plants can die from being planted too low (tomatoes are an exception). If the soil does need a lot of work, dig a big hole (incorporating some of the original soil) but place the plant on a hard center to keep it above the soil line.

Pruning Tips:

- Pruning encourages new growth, which is dangerous if the new shoots are hit with frost.

- Prune root tips (not more than a third) and some of the limbs before a plant is transplanted. This works even better if the pruning is performed a year in advance of the move.

- In renewal pruning, the oldest branches are cut at ground level, leaving only younger vigorous growth. Be careful with trees and shrubs – they should be pruned gradually over a few years.

- To reduce plant size, cut out undesirable longer limbs from inside the plant. Do not cut all branches the same length

- A formal hedge should be pruned to allow light penetration into the center of the plant. Strive for a pyramidal form, the base is wider than the top. With this method, the lower branches do not become shaded and spindly.

PRUNING HEDGES

RIGHT
This type of pruning gives solid growth at the base.

WRONG
This type of pruning destroys bottom growth and gives a top-heavy appearance.

PRUNING PARTICULARS:

- **Plants that bloom after June 1** (summer blooming): Prune in late winter or very early spring, before the new growth begins. They set bloom buds on new wood in spring for summer or fall. Examples: crape myrtle, gardenia, white hydrangea.

- **Camellias (& roses)** will have bigger blooms if competing flower buds are removed. When there are many buds on a stem, it is best to pinch off some of the buds to encourage the others.

- **Plants that bloom before June 1** (Spring blooming) should be pruned immediately after flowering. They develop their blooms during the growing season. Examples: azalea, camellia, daphne, forsythia.

- **Evergreen shrubs** can be lightly pruned anytime to maintain their shape, but heavy pruning should be done in late winter before new growth.

- **Nandinas** and other plants that grow from a central crown: Cut the oldest canes to the ground. Prune about a third each year.

- **Cedar, hemlock, juniper:** Do not prune the branches past the green foliage.

- **Berry-producing plants** produce on older branches. Remove one third of old growth each year after the fruit drops. Examples: holly and pyracantha.

- **French hydrangeas** (blue, pink) may be pruned after bloom in July or August. Since they bloom on old wood, any major pruning should be done gradually over a period of years.

- **Oleaners:** Prune in late summer after bloom.

- **Climbing roses:** Prune after bloom.

- **Dogwoods:** Prune after their leaves are fully formed. Because they are "bleeders", they should be pruned a little each year, and not all at once.

- **Prune after bloom is a good general rule.**

Month-to-Month

December is a month for celebration. Enjoy decorating your home with greenery and berries from your garden. Southern tradition calls for wreaths, garlands, swags and table arrangements filled with fragrant foliage and seasonal fruits. Seedpods, cones, feathers and dried flowers can be added for a special touch.

PLANT:

- Tulips may be taken out of the refrigerator and planted this month. It is not too late to plant other spring flowering bulbs.

- Hardy annuals and perennials may still be planted.

- Shrubs and trees may still be planted. Keep them well watered to protect from freezing temperatures. Established plants, including those from the woods, may be moved this month.

- Transplant deciduous trees. Plant camellias.

- Consider purchasing a living Christmas Tree that can be planted outside later. Be careful that the variety you select can tolerate our summer heat.

- Rye grass can still be sown this month.

PRUNE:

- Prune overgrown hollies by cutting top branches to mere stubs; leave lower branches longer.

- Prune boxwood by cutting out branches to let light inside.

- Crape myrtles can be pruned. Remember less pruning is more! Thou shalt not commit Crape murder!

- Prune berried plants and greens for Christmas decorations. Prune dead wood from plants.

Winter

FERTILIZE:
- Feed dormant trees and shrubs.

- Fertilize rye grass that has been over seeded.

- Keep feeding pansies with a liquid 20-20-20 in December and January between spells of especially cold weather. After heavy frosts pinching off dead flowers helps plants recover with healthy new blossom formation.

- Yellow leaves on camellias may indicate tea scale. Treat with dormant oil spray when temperatures are above freezing.

BLOOMING:
- Holly, nandina, pyracantha, acuba, camellia, japonica, narcissus, ornamental cabbage, pansy, alyssum, tea olive.

DECEMBER TIPS:
- Cover lilies of the valley with compost for more blooms.

- Begin organizing garden catalogs and fill out orders.

- If a freeze is forecast, water well to prevent damage. Susceptible plants may be covered with cloth or heavily mulched, but the covering should be removed as it begins to warm, lest further damage occur from the rapid warming.

- Protect container plantings by grouping them together and using protective covering if necessary.

- Protect tender **perennials** with thick mulch of straw.

When you take a flower in your hand and really look at it, it is your world for the moment.

— Georgia O'Keeffe

Poinsettias should be placed in good light, out of the way of drafts. They should be watered well about twice a week (when the dirt feels dry). Poinsettias may be used as cut flowers. The leaves should be stripped and the cut stems placed in hot water for conditioning. When the plant has finished blooming it may be planted outside on the sunny south side of the house. In this location it will bloom each year.

Buy your **Christmas tree** as soon as they appear in the lots. Remove 2 inches from the trunk and place tree in a bucket of water, in shade until you're ready for it. Water tree daily with warm water throughout the season.

When cutting **greenery** for holiday decorations, remember that you are pruning the plant. Remove a branch at its base where it intersects another limb rather that snipping it in half. Also cut at an angle above a node.

POINSETTIA CARE

With proper care your Christmas poinsettia can be kept to enjoy again next Christmas. Continue watering it normally until the first of April. Then gradually let it dry out until the middle of May. Then cut the stems back to about four inches above the soil and repot it in new soil. Water thoroughly and place in a sunny location without letting the plant get overheated or becoming too dry. When new growth appears, fertilize every two weeks. In June move the pot outside into a lightly shaded location. Continue watering and fertilizing. Pinch the stems back one inch in early July and again in late August, leaving three or four leaves on each shoot. Then bring the plant indoors and place it in a sunny window. Keep an even temperature of about 65 to 75 degrees and continue to water and fertilize. Be sure to place the plant in total darkness between 5 p.m. and 8 a.m. from the first of October until Thanksgiving. Continue feeding the plant until mid-December. You will be rewarded with beautiful colorful leaves to thank you for your efforts.

The poinsettia is named for Joel Poinsett (1779-1851) from Charleston, S.C. He brought home many exotic plants from his foreign travels. The poinsettia is from Mexico.

GREAT GIFTS FOR AND FROM GARDENERS:

- A subscription to a gardening magazine, or the Master Gardener Calendar.

- A gift certificate to have their tools sharpened. Check with garden centers. Gardeners can always use sharp clippers.

- Volunteer to help weed. Pulling weeds can be therapeutic – just ask our volunteers at the Woodrow Wilson House.

- A trip to the Riverbanks Botanical Garden or any of the gardens listed in this book. (Remember your camera.)

- Hire a gardening service for a day to help with big tasks, such as pruning.

- Photograph their garden, (have the film put on a CD) and have the photos made into notecards.

- Share your garden: Pass along plants, seeds or bulbs. Include planting directions and present them in a decorative basket. Dry seeds and place in small plastic bags with growing instructions and a picture cut from a plant catalog.

- Air dry herbs by hanging bunches with rubber bands onto wire coat hangers. Hang them in a warm, airy place. When dry, tie with a ribbon to decorate presents. Dry herbs can also be placed in a small bag with a good recipe featuring that herb.

- Use dried herbs to make scented pillows, sachets, wreaths and potpourri.

Winter

January is the preparation month. Most of the country cannot garden year round but we who live in paradise will have some wonderful late fall – early spring days to enjoy the garden. But during those days when the weather is bad, have fun studying your garden catalogs and making plans for spring. As you walk around your garden, clean up dead limbs and leaves that have accumulated, so that when things begin to bloom (sooner rather than later), their setting will be neat and will not attract disease.

PLANT:
- Continue to plant perennial herbs and cool weather annual herbs such as chives, fennel, dill, asparagus through February.

- Sow poppies, larkspur seeds into ground. Sweet peas are best if started from seeds after Thanksgiving. First soak the seeds in water over night. Then plant in prepared soil with mushroom compost. Plant about an inch deep and cover with pine straw. You may need to protect them from rabbits.

- Plant or transplant trees and shrubs.

PRUNE:
- Prune grape vines.

- Avoid pruning plants that seem damaged by freezing. Wait until spring and see if they bud then prune as needed.

- May need to pinch back leggy annuals to promote flowering.

- Prune out old canes on oleander.

FERTILIZE:
- Fertilize pecan trees - add 4 lbs/per inch of trunk diameter of 8-8-8 or 10-10-10 along the drip line to encourage nuts.

- Feed pansies with liquid fertilizer every 10-14 days and deadhead spent blooms.

- Lime gerbera daises. But do not lime acid-loving plants like camellias, iris and azaleas.

BLOOMING:
- Camellia, pansy, snapdragons, daphne, quince

TIPS:
- Remember to "Grind the Greens," which is to dispose of your cut Christmas tree in a thoughtful manner.

- Clean under camellias- remove spent blooms that could encourage petal blight. Remove buds that seem too crowded and the remaining blooms will be more vigorous.

- Protect tender plants from cold damage. When freezing weather is predicted, water plants because frozen soil cannot supply moisture to the leaves. Keep plants well mulched.

- Prepare flowerbeds, if dry. Add compost, manure or other organic matter and till to 6"-8" deep.

- Apply a pre-emergent herbicide such as Dacthal on your lawn to kill seeds of crabgrass and broadleaf weeds as they germinate

- Treat hydrangeas with aluminum sulphate to obtain blue flowers or lime or super-phosphate to make them pink

- Roses need to be ordered now. If roses tempt you, remember that they need to be sprayed with chemicals weekly because they are susceptible to diseases. Hybrid roses are an enormous amount of work. Old roses, on the other hand, require far less maintenance.

The man who has planted a garden has done something good for the world.

February is a wonderful month to continue getting your garden ready for spring. In Columbia, on some days you can feel spring in the air. No winter blues here. Pruning and planting should be the big items on your agenda, along with daily walks around your yard just to enjoy all the beginning blooms that signal the end of winter. Carry pruners in the garden and trim broken or misplaced branches.

PLANT:

It is a good time to move plants to different locations if changes are desired. Trees and shrubs can still be planted now. This will allow roots to become somewhat established before top growth begins. Always dig a hole larger (wider is more important than deep) than the roots. Work in organic matter if needed. If the plant is bare rooted, place the roots over a cone of dirt. Never place the plant too low. Fill in with soil and water well. Mulch.

- Plant tulip bulbs. Plant lily of the valley in shade.

- Nasturtiums may be sown in the outside soil.

- Start perennial seeds on your window sill.

- Plant violas, sweet William, English daisy, alyssum

- Roses should be planted this month. You must have a well drained, sunny location, and you must prepare the ground adequately with organic material, fertilizer and lime. Proper preparation will ensure years of pleasure.

- Divide and replant perennials, ferns, and ground covers. Share with other gardeners or potential gardeners.

I send a little flower,
My messenger to be;
Let it whisper in thine ear
All I would say to thee.

~ Old Valentine Verse

PRUNE:

- Heavy pruning for size and shape may be accomplished this month on all but spring flowering shrubs and trees. Prune out all dead, injured and diseased branches. Remove unsightly shoots at the base. Prune out long branches deep within the body of the plant to obtain a natural look.

- Prune roses between early- February and mid- March. Canes less than the diameter of a pencil and all inward growing or crossing canes should be removed to the bud union. Remove dead, dying and weak canes. Leave 4-8 healthy canes. Prune climbing roses after the first flush of spring bloom, since they produce flowers on the previous year's growth.

- Crape myrtle and other summer bloomers can be pruned this month, if not pruned earlier in winter. But please don't over prune crape myrtles. They bloom on new growth and may benefit from a winter pruning including removal of some of the old flower heads.

- Do **NOT** prune spring- flowering trees and shrubs such as spirea, azalea, dogwood and flowering quince until after blooming.

- Cut or mow established mondo and liriope before new growth appears. Use clippers, string trimmer or set mower to three inches. In about two months you will have a fresh green border.

- Thin out annual seeds like larkspur, poppies, sweet peas.

- Prune evergreen shrubs.

FEBRUARY PRUNING TIPS:

The best time of the year to prune "stone" fruits is February – not in the fall. Apple, pear, and cherry trees are best maintained in a Christmas tree shape with a central leader and 45-degree angle spread of branches every 30 inches. Peach, nectarine and plum trees are best trained to an open center. Remove dead and unproductive branches on blueberry bushes now and cut old ones to encourage growth. Limit the size of fruit trees by cutting off some of the new growth each year. Prune out any shoots that are crossed, broken, or diseased.

February

FERTILIZE:

- Be careful about general fertilizing at this time. Do not encourage new growth, which may be hurt by freezing temperatures.

- Lime gerbera daises. But do not lime acid loving plants like camellias, iris, azaleas.

- Feed iris with bone meal, lightly top dress with wood ashes.

- As you see perennials peeking out, you may fertilize as they are starting to grow and need nutrients. Be careful not to fertilize before the last hard freeze.

- Fertilize bulbs with 5-10-10 as foliage appears.

- Fertilize pansies every 10-14 days using a liquid fertilizer or a time-release fertilizer.

- Lime sulphur may be applied to roses and other plants to kill dormant insects and disease spores. Spray around the mulch as well as the plants.

- Dormant oil spray may be applied now, if not done in January. Follow label directions. This will help control disease on camellias.

BLOOMING:

- Camellia, Japanese magnolia, creeping rosemary, forsythia, daffodil, crocus, candytuft, violet, pansy, dianthus, flowering quince, evergreen clematis, daphne odora, tea olive, winter and carolina jasmine, lenten rose. *It's great to live in the South!*

FEBRUARY TIPS:

- Take soil sample now if you have not done one in the last few years because soil amendments such as lime takes time to become effective. You should re-evaluate your soil periodically.

- Feed the birds and make sure they have fresh water.

- As camellias bloom, clean up spent blooms to help prevent insects and diseases.

- Enjoy spring blooms early inside your home by forcing any woody plant that has flower buds. Crush stem ends, strip lower leaves, and put into warm water in a cool, bright spot. Try forsythia, quince, winter jasmine, and pussy willow.

- Yard tools (especially pruners) should be sharpened and oiled to prepare for spring. Mark handles with colored tape or paint, so they won't get lost in the beds.

- Cover marginally hardy plants with burlap, leaves or baskets if a freeze is predicted. Remember to remove as temperatures rise. You may also need to protect tender new growth on plants.

Compared to gardeners, I think it is generally agreed that others understand very little about anything of consequence.

~ Henry Mitchell

March into the garden. It is time to get to work. The days are starting to get longer and there is valuable time now for planting. Your summer gardening chores depend on what you do now. Don't forget – for every weed you pull now you are preventing 100 summer weeds from forming. And it's time to pull those volunteer tiny trees before they become bigger and so much tougher. The average last frost in mid-Carolina is mid-April.

PLANT:

- Remember to protect tender plants from frost.

- Most cuttings will root in water. It is an ideal time to root African violets, azaleas, and most houseplants.

- Perennials can now be dug, divided and replanted. Examples include asters, coreopsis, mums, iris, daylilies, shasta daisies and grasses.

- Set out dormant, bare-root roses. Prune rose bushes except spring-blooming climbers.

- Plant perennial bedding plants like gerbera daises, pinks, shasta daises, coreopsis, & perennial salvia.

- **Annuals:** When buying, bigger isn't always better. Choose the branched plant that is well proportioned, not the tall one that has become root-bound. Transplants without flowers are better (but, it is nice to confirm the blooms colors), and a younger plant is a better than an older, stressed one. Watch out for signs of insects or disease. It is acceptable and smart to gently pull shrubs from their pots to check out the roots.

- It is a good time to start seeds indoors, like morning glories, nasturtiums (soak seeds overnight in water), portulaca, & cleome. Start zinnia seeds and continue planting at intervals for cut flowers in fall.

> *No matter what changes take place in the world, or in me, nothing ever seems to disturb the face of spring.*
>
> – E. B. White

PRUNE:

- Prune spring-flowering shrubs and trees soon after they bloom.

- *Summer flowering shrubs* (those that bloom after June) should be pruned now. They bloom on new wood, so pruning now forces new growth, which will produce more blooms. Do not shear plants and make boxes or mounds; keep them natural looking. Cut to control shape and size.

- Crape myrtles can still be shaped now, but do not prune severely.

- Evergreens can still be pruned in early March, provided new growth has not begun.

- Cut ivy back severely. It may look "naked" – but it will soon "put out" and not get out of bounds, as ivy can often do.

- Pinch back tall, leggy plants to improve their shape.

- Trim overgrown or cold damaged gardenias. Remove entire branch at the origination point to avoid a pruned look. Feed with a slow-release fertilizer that contains iron as well as other minor elements, such as zinc, boron, and manganese.

- Prune roses (if not done in February). Always make a cut above a bud facing outward.

MARCH TIPS:

- For snails and slugs: Mix about three tablespoons of Epsom salt to one gallon of water and pour on area.

- Aphids: Curling leaves are a clue that these sap-sucking pests have arrived. Tender new leaves often attract aphids. Many plants will outgrow the problem. Good predators, such as ladybugs and praying mantis, may intervene for you. If the problem continues, spray with insecticidal soap or Malathion.

March

FERTILIZE:

- Feed azalea, rhododendron and laurel just after they bloom. Use azalea/camellia and rhododendron food (for all acid loving plants) 4-10-10. Do not feed too early because it will cause blooms to "blast" (bloom too early and fall off). Spread fertilizer evenly over the surface of soil around bush, a bit beyond the spread of branches, and thoroughly water into the ground. Never cultivate soil under the branches because the feeding roots are very near the surface and can be easily damaged. Mulch with peat, pine needles, or leafmold.

- Fertilize roses as soon as new growth appears.

- Fertilize perennials now and divide clumps of perennials that have become too large.

- Apply 10-6-6 or similar granular fertilizer to shrubs at a rate of 1/2 tablespoon per foot of plant height.

- Fertilize camellias after blooming and again in six weeks.

- Mid-March is the last date to apply pre-emergent herbicides. Lime can still be added if needed.

- Keep feeding pansies every 10-14 days with liquid fertilizer. And keep dead heading.

BLOOMING:

- Camellia, lenten rose, some spring bulbs, violet, pansy, dianthus, quince, daphne, tea olive, jasmine, snapdragon

SOWING SEEDS IN FLATS OUTDOORS
Soil preparation:
Use a mix that is loose and drains well but retains moisture. Screen mix through 1/2 inch mesh. Treat seeding mixture with a fungicide or start seeds in vermiculite. For containers, use any pot, box, or pan that has drainage holes.

How to sow:
Fill the container to 1/2 to 3/4 inch from the top with the soil mix, and press firmly with your hand. Mark off the rows with a ruler, pressing it 1/4 inch deep into the mix. Space the rows 2 inches apart. Sow the seeds in the furrows and cover with sand or sifted peat moss. Firm again so there is a good contact between seed and soil. Water carefully with a fine mist or soak the seed containers from the bottom. Cover with wet newspaper and a pane of glass. Place in a warm spot but not in direct sun. Keep the soil moist, but not soaking, at all times. Check regularly for germination.

When seeds germinate, remove the covering and place in a brighter light. Lift the seedlings when they have developed two sets of true leaves, and move them to larger flats. Space them about 1 1/2 inches apart. Keep watering! Gradually expose to more sun. Plants may be set out in the garden in 4 to 5 weeks.

ROOTING GERANIUMS
Geraniums are hard to start from seed and usually expensive if bought as plants. So...buy several small or one medium-sized plant which can easily be found during March. Look for a plant with as many branches as possible for cuttings. With a sharp knife, cut diagonally above joints, leaves, or growth nodes. Get a limb no less than 1 1/2 inches. Wet the base of this cutting shaking off excess moisture. Dip in a root-stimulating hormone powder. Stick this cutting into a wet fertile cube or some other sterile medium. Place in an airtight plastic bag, first in the shade (a day or two) then in the sun. Roots should appear in 7 to 14 days. Then plant in a pot. For the price of one plant you now have 3 to 5 new ones.

April: It's beautiful and feels great to be outside, so get out and get dirty. It is a busy month for gardening. Mid-April is a pretty reliable last frost date for mid South Carolina.

PLANT:

- The planting area must be well prepared. With hot weather coming, attention must be given to keeping new plants well watered and mulched.

- This is the opportune time to plant warm season annuals, perennials, shrubs and trees. But, it is beginning to get too late in the spring to plant bare-root stock. Try new varieties and new color combinations. Check under leaves for insects and insect eggs before purchasing plants.

- Seeds of heat-loving annuals such as zinnia, marigold, portulaca, rudbeckia, gloriosa daisy and celosia may be sown where they are to grow, or plants from garden centers may planted. In the shade try begonias, impatiens, ageratum, among ferns or hosta. Water well unless rainfall is adequate. You will have bushier, stronger plants if you can make yourself pinch off all blooms and buds from the new plants at planting time.

- Dahlias and canna lilies may be planted this month for summer bloom. In full sun, dahlias will give rich color well into the fall. Newly introduced varieties of cannas are very attractive especially for foliage and now they are offered in differing heights.

- Plant summer-flowering bulbs: Plant clematis. Caladiums may be started from tubers.

- In some instances like heavy shade or a rocky area, the only option for ground cover may be moss. To make, puree some moss in a blender with three parts beer to one part sugar. (Buttermilk can also be an additive) Spread the mixture and mist with water often.

Another name for the little viola, Johnny Jump Up, is "Meet her in the entry, kiss her in the buttery"

- Plant basil, dill and other annual herbs.

- Climbing roses require little pruning – only cut out old, diseased or dead wood. If you train new canes of climbers horizontally and low you will get maximum bloom. They can make a neglected spot into a place of beauty. Every garden should have a Lady Banksia Rose.

- Plant gladiolas at two-week intervals to extend flowering.

- Start hanging baskets early in April. Impatiens, begonias and caladiums do well in the shade. For sunny locations try verbena, trailing lantana, dwarf marigold, annual vinca, portulaca and petunias. For a bushier basket, keep the plant tips pinched. Also start pots for your patio. See container gardening in this book.

- Chrysanthemums should be rooted and replanted or divided. When new shoots have reached five inches long, cut below a leaf node. Remove the lower leaves and dip the stem in rooting hormone. Place in sand or sterile potting medium up to, but not touching, the top leaves. These should root in ten to twenty days. After that, plant in your garden and fertilize after two weeks. Pinch for bushier growth when six inches tall and continue pinching until August 1. Though this is standard practice, some gardeners in our area note two to three bloom periods if the chrysanthemums are cut back after flowering each time and kept fertilized.

PRUNE:
- Finish pruning evergreens and summer-flowering shrubs, it is about too late.

- Cut back the stems of daffodils so the flowers do not produce seed. Do not cut back the foliage, as it is now storing food.

- Azaleas or oak leaf hydrangeas can be pruned after blooming. To keep at present height, prune about one third. If they are overgrown cut back two or three of the largest stems to the base. Prune other stems to just below the desired height. Prune forsythia, quince, spirea, and other spring flowering shrubs in the same way. Never shear the shrubs as it destroys their natural graceful growth pattern.

April

- Pyracantha is prized for its winter berries and the birds it attracts, including flocks of Cedar Waxwings. Its growth, however, may be difficult to contain. Protect yourself from the thorns using good heavy gloves. Prune out all long and wayward shoots now, so that the remaining limbs will develop the colorful berries.

- Shear hardy candytuft, alyssum and lobelia after blooming. This makes it look neater and provides a succession of bloom. Deadhead snapdragons for more flowers. The blooms will be smaller but they do provide garden color. Continue this procedure, along with fertilization, for repeat bloom, until the plants are killed by hot weather.

FERTILIZE:

- Now is a good time to add a layer of compost. (Buy by the truckload at Dixie Landscaping Supply in Lexington.) A good mix is mushroom compost and bark grind. This serves as mulch, too.

- Fertilize boxwood and other shrubs with 10-10-10 or a slower acting 16-4-8. Fertilize emerging perennials lightly.

- Inspect roses often and control aphids and disease with sprays at 7-10 day intervals, increasing to 10-14 day intervals when weather gets hotter.

- Begin a lawn fertilization program this month after green-up. Sod lawn if needed. Warm-season grasses can be planted now through July.

- If your garden needs calcium, use recycled ground eggshells or oyster shells. They are also a deterrent to slugs or snails.

Flowers are the sweetest things God ever made and forgot to put a soul into.

— Henry Ward Beeche

- If slugs are getting into your pots, hotglue pennies two rows high around the bottom of the pot. Copper shocks slugs.

- If you have not fertilized your azaleas, you must do so now. Use azalea-camellia fertilizer on azaleas, camellias, and daylilies. Use one tablespoon per foot of plant height. Spread it lightly beneath and beyond the branches. Do not throw it at the base. Water well. You may repeat this again in May and then in early July.

- You may still spray shrubs for tea scale, but be sure to do it before temperatures go above 80 degrees. Use a mixture of Volck oil and an insecticide as recommended by the county extension agent or nurseryman. This spray will also control other scales as well as red spiders. It may be used on most garden shrubs, but should be used particularly on azaleas, camellias, yaupon, boxwood, hollies and gardenias, as they are more susceptible to scale. Systemic insecticides may be used at any temperature, but not on plants grown for fruit or vegetables. Be careful of over-spraying on adjacent plants.

BLOOMING:
- Azalea, Lady Banksia Rose, oakleaf hydrangea, camellia, roses, spirea, dogwood, bradford pear, jasmine, alyssum, johnny-jump-up, amaryllis, lantana, larkspur, nasturtium, pansy, petunia, snapdragon, iris.

APRIL TIPS:
- Divide asters when weather permits.

- To revitalize your houseplants move them out under the trees for the summer. This is a good time to repot container plants

- Don't wait until your flowers topple over to stake them. Choose a staking method that will support the plant without detracting from its appearance. As the plant grows, its stake should become almost invisible. Manufactured stakes and cages are available at garden centers and through the mail. One of the simplest and most unobtrusive methods is to use some twiggy branches of durable wood, such as dogwood or azalea, about 6 inches shorter than the ultimate height of the plant you stake.

April

- Give yourself a treat: visit local garden centers and farmer's markets to check out new plants. Keep lists of all the plants you buy and where you plant them. Note blooming times and performance in your journal. Take pictures to help you remember what each bed looks like this spring (and also take pictures at other seasons). Keep notes at the back of this book.

- Avoid big pots for geraniums. Large roomy pots encourage a profusion of leaves instead of a profusion of flowers. Use medium size pots instead.

- Check out your irrigation system to see if it works properly. Use soaker hoses in flower boarders. Overhead sprinkler systems are fine for turf grass, but most flowers and vegetables do better with a watering system that puts water right at the roots and not on the leaves.

- Begin to pinch mums monthly until August

- Daffodils need their foliage to grow for 12 weeks after flowering.

- Dig up overgrown cannas, and divide remaining plants.

TOMATO TIPS:

- Plant now but watch weather for that odd frost.
- The soil temp should be at least 50 degrees.
- Plant tomatoes deeply.
- Some of the best plants for large fruits are: Better Boy, Park's Whopper and Celebrity.
- Some of the best cherry tomato plants are: Sweet 100, Small Fry, and Cherry Grande.
- Paste type tomatoes are: Roma VF and UC 82.
- Plants grow best at average air temperatures between 70-75 degrees.
- Look for "VFN" on the plant labels, which indicates they are bred to resist diseases.
- Transplants can be rooted from a healthy young shoot of your early planting.
- Rotate where you plant tomatoes to avoid insects & diseases.
- Place the plants at least 5 feet apart, so insects do not spread.
- Folear-feed (spray the leaves of plants) every two weeks. But do not give them too much nitrogen, or you'll get beautiful leaves and no fruit.
- Hold off on fertilizing once the plant begins to flower.
- The following plants in your tomato patch may ward off disease, encourage growth and improve flavor: leaf lettuce, nasturtiums, parsley, onions, chives, and marigolds.
- Do not plant tomatoes with cabbage, fennel, or potatoes.
- Concrete wire makes strong, tall tomato cages, and the holes are big enough for hands at harvesting.
- Do mulch. Even though they are a summer crop they do suffer from too much heat, especially their roots.
- Protect plants from birds or cutworms by wrapping a 2 inch wide piece of aluminum foil around the stem so that it is about an inch above the ground and an inch below.
- When watering, try not to get the leaves wet. Use a soaker hose. When the fruit begins to ripen, cut back on water.
- If you do use a sprinkler system, then water in the morning so the sun and wind can dry the plants.
- Remove diseased leaves. Especially watch the lower leaves for leaf spots.
- Calcium makes the tomato stems stronger.
- Tomatoes can be harvested approximately 70-80 days after planting.
- Harvest fruit when fully ripe for the best flavor.

Spring

May: It has started to get a little warm and planting slows down. Maintenance, care and feeding become of great importance.

PLANT:

- Plant an extra row of vegetables or herbs for our hungry neighbors. For information call Harvest Hope Food Bank at (803) 765-9181 in Columbia S.C.

- Complete spring planting; it is getting too hot and dry.

- Container-grown shrubs can continue to be planted. Consider adding some fragrant varieties near windows and patios. Air layering of forsythia can be done now.

- Warm-season grasses can be planted.

- Plant rooted chrysanthemums where you wish them to bloom in the fall. Root stem cuttings, if you did not do it in April.

- Do not forget to plant biennials, forget-me-nots, scotch thistle, English daisy, sweet Williams, Iceland poppies and salvia sclera; plant them in a nursery bed in the summer and move them to a final location the following spring. Many will self-sow.

- Plant a tree to mark weddings, anniversaries, birthdays or Mother's Day.

- Interplant herbs among ornamentals for accents.

- Day lilies are beginning to bloom. Make your selections while you can see the blooms and plant them this month. Clumps are easily lifted, divided and transplanted now.

> *It is only to the gardener that time is a friend, giving each year more than he steals.*
>
> — Beverley Nichols

- Caladium tubers like the warm ground. Plant them now. Dahlias also may be planted at this time.

- It is a good time to start popular native wildflowers from seed.

- Plant caladiums and continue planting gladiolas every 2 weeks until 2 months before first frost.

PRUNE:
- Prune azaleas, forsythia, weigela and quinceshrubs immediately after they flower. Remember, you don't have to prune unless you need to correct form, reduce size or cut out dead or diseased wood.

- Bulb foliage needs to mature and yellow before it is removed so the bulbs will flower again next spring. To help conceal the unattractive foliage overplant with annuals such as wax begonia or marigold.

- Roses – trim climbers as they finish spring blooming. Remove dead or weak wood as needed. Shorten long healthy canes by about 1/3 and secure to trellis.

- Ferns and other heavy feeders such as tropicals require a weekly dose of liquid food like 20-20-20. Ferns are looking forward to a spring-cleaning, so be certain to overhaul (cut out old foliage) them early, allowing room for the new vigorous growth to follow.

FERTILIZE:
- Shrubs need the second application of fertilizer now. Use a balanced fertilizer, one tablespoon per foot of height for shrubs or one cup per inch of trunk diameter for trees as in March.

- Give day lilies a light application of fertilizer as the buds begin to appear. Flower substance and bloom will be improved with irrigation in the absence of rainfall.

May

- After blooming, fertilize iris with a balanced fertilizer or well rotted cow manure. Do not touch rhizome with fertilizer.

- Crape myrtles may be fertilized now if not done earlier. Use one half cup per inch of trunk diameter spread beneath and beyond the branches.

- Fertilize azaleas and camellias as they finish blooming.

- Fertilize roses monthly

INSECTS & DISEASES:

Keep your eyes open for signs of insects and be prepared to spray. Yellow foliage may be caused by lace bugs and spider mites. A brownish deposit on the underside of leaves and a small insect with lacy wings indicates lace bug. A fine webbing can suggest spider mites. Aphids are tiny round, usually green insects found on a new growth. Most insects may be controlled with an insecticide spray or dust. Use carefully according to manufacturer's directions. Use a commercial-type spreader, or a small amount of detergent in the spray so that the spray will not be washed off with the first shower. Spider mites may be more difficult to control. Junipers are especially susceptible to these. A miticide must be used for control. A hard spray of cold water also dislodges them. With high humidity fungal diseases may become a problem. They may be controlled with a fungicide.

If using a program of regular spraying, keep roses sprayed at seven to ten day intervals. Use a dust or spray especially formulated for roses. It should contain a fungicide to control black spot as well as an insecticide.

Here is an environmentally safe way to control slugs: rinse eggshells and let them dry. Crush them into very small pieces and sprinkle them on the soil around the plants. They will repel slugs. The shells will gradually decompose adding calcium to the soil.

Spring unlocks the flowers to paint the laughing soil.

— Reginald Heber

If your camellias are heavily infested with scale (indicated by a white deposit on the underside of the leaves), they may be drenched or sprayed every six weeks with a systemic insecticide as recommended. Follow directions carefully. You may also need to treat with dormant oil. Treat the problem completely.

Inspect gardenias for white flies. Spray with insecticide soap as needed.

BLOOMING:
- Magnolia, oakleaf hydrangea, rose, shasta daisy, blue salvia, iris, larkspur, pansy, dianthus, poppy, gerbera daisy, stokesia, verbena, yarrow (pink), snapdragon.

For winter's rains and ruins are over...
Blossom by blossom the spring begins.

— Algernon Charles Swinburne

MAY TIPS:

- If there is not adequate rain, water your beds and lawn well once a week applying at least 1/2 to 1 inch of water. Early morning watering is preferred.

- After the Easter lily flowers fade, plant them in the garden, in a sunny, well-drained spot. Leave the foliage to encourage the bulbs' growth.

- To conserve moisture and decrease weeds, mulch shrubs and flowers. Use pine straw, hay, oak leaves or compost to a depth of two to three inches. But do not pile up against the trunks. Mulch all plants except some iris (bearded, tectorum, cristata.)

- Pinch back phlox, asters and mums to encourage bushy plants.

- Keep newly-planted trees and shrubs well watered.

- Severely deadhead geraniums, annuals, roses, and perennials before leaving town for more than two weeks.

- Water newly-planted material. Pay close attention to fast-draining areas near walls, walkways and patios. Plants should never be stressed because of lack of water during the first year. And then the challenge: do not over-water either.

- Begin to stake or encircle perennials, which tend to get tall and fall over in wind or rain.

- Dry herbs from your garden now.

- **Bees:** When cutting flowers, don't be caught unaware by sleeping bees. In early morning or late evening you may find the little stingers napping. As soon as the sun warms the air, they'll wake up and fly away. Just don't get stung in the meantime.

LAWNS IN MAY:

- Proper mowing height is the best weed control. A taller mowing height will also help your lawn survive dry weather. Leaving well-chopped grass clippings on the lawn releases significant amounts of nitrogen and potassium which add nutrients to the lawn.

- To encourage grass to grow in difficult areas, thin trees and remove lower limbs (except magnolias – they create too much shade for any grass) so that three or four hours of daily sunlight reach the turf.

- Feed warm season grasses, such as zoysia, bermuda and st. augustine with 6 pounds of 16-4-8 per 1,000 sq. feet of lawn. Use a slow release formula so it doesn't release at one time and wash off with first rain.

- Fertilize centipede during the beginning of May, with a ratio like 15-0-15 or 16-4-8.

- Now is the time to aerate and de thatch warm season grasses.

- Aerate after dormancy and before the weather gets too hot.

Oh, Adam was a gardener, and God who made him sees that half a proper gardener's work is done upon his knees. So when your work is finished, you can wash your hands and pray, for the glory of the garden that it may not pass away!

– Rudyard Kipling

June is the time to enjoy your garden, find a shady spot and create a personal relaxation spot. A simple bench or even a log will do. For a table, try a few bricks with a marble tile on top. Decorating is not only for interiors. Make a conversational sitting area. Also prepare a meditation area (near a water feature is great), "meditation area" sounds better than "secret hide-out place."

PLANT:
- Anything planted now may require extra water and care.

- **Annuals:** It's not too late to sow zinnia, marigold and cosmos seeds, but be sure to protect the young seedlings from the sun until they are established.

- **Perennials:** Set out summer and fall-blooming perennials now for a late-season display. Good choices include perennial salvia, purple coneflower, asters, helianthus, and Japanese anemones. Water thoroughly after planting.

- Build children's enthusiasm for gardening by preparing a small plot with rich soil in an area with lots of sun. Plant large-seeded flowers such as four-o'clock's, zinnias, or sunflowers. They're easy, fast growing and fun.

- **Tomatoes:** Plant young tomato plants early and late for a harvest that continues into fall. If tomato plants are not available, root cuttings from established plants.

- Quick-growing annual vines such as moon-flower or morning glory can be planted on trellises.

*Summer afternoon - summer afternoon;
to me those have always been the two most
beautiful words in the English language.*

— Henry James

PRUNE:

- Pinch out the top set of new leaves on annuals. This results in a bushier plant with more blossoms.

- Prune tips of mums and dahlias every three weeks until mid-August for bushier growth and blooms.

- Remove fading and dead flowers from plants. This keeps the plant from putting its energy into seed instead of bloom, and keeps the garden neat.

FERTILIZE:
- Use bloom-buster type fertilizer to keep those annuals blooming.

- Fertilize crape myrtles. Buy now to check color.

BLOOMING:
- Day lilies, annuals, roses, iris, gardenias, magnolia, hydrangea, oleander, rhododendron, hibiscus, Japanese iris, lantana, plumbago and mimosa trees.

JUNE TIPS:
- A good slow soaking at ground level once a week is more beneficial to your plants than frequent light sprinklings, especially from above. This encourages mildew. The best time to water is in the morning, between 5 a.m. and 8 a.m. Mulch to retain moisture and discourage weeds.

- Careful, this is Japanese Beetle Month!

- Do not forget fresh water for birds, especially in hot, dry weather

- Repel mosquitoes by putting some water in a white dinner plate and add just a couple of drops of Lemon Fresh Joy dishwashing soap. Set the dish away from people. It attracts the bugs and they die. Works great!

July: The most important concern for plants in our area in July is water. So supplement the dry periods with deep watering, thickly mulch everything, and watch for too much sun. Remember to treat yourself as you do your favorite plants – drink plenty of water, use sunscreen and rest in the shade.

PLANT:
- Plant quick-growing annuals now for fall color: ageratum, cosmos, marigold, zinnia. You will have fall cut flowers.

- Sow seeds of next year's biennials now through August. Canterbury bells, foxglove and sweet William in mid-July; pansies, English daises, and forget-me-nots in August.

PRUNE:
- Remove fading and dead flower heads.

- Remove annuals past their prime. Replant with quick growing, heat-loving flowers such as marigolds, zinnias, salvia, portulaca, periwinkle and asters.

- Cut back dahlias about halfway, give them light fertilizing, and get ready to enjoy fall blooms.

- Remove the flower clusters of crape myrtles as soon as the petals fall. (But do leave some for the birds to eat.) This prolongs blooming. Fertilize with 8-8-8.

- Pinch back chrysanthemums until mid-July. Feed monthly with a balanced fertilizer according to package directions.

- Mow lawns frequently and high. Never take off more than one inch during the summer months. Raise your mower blade 1/2 inch if necessary. Maintain a regular lawn mowing schedule.

FERTILIZE:

- Apply liquid fertilizer regularly to annuals.

- Feed your lawn (if it is zoysia, bermuda or st. augustine) this month with 8-8-8 fertilizer. If the soil is dry, water the day before you fertilize and immediately after. Fertilize centipede mid-summer, with a ratio like 15-0-15 or 16-4-8.

- Give roses a mid-summer feeding of 1/4 cup rose fertilizer per plant.

BLOOMING:

- Many annuals: zinnia, marigold, cosmos, impatiens, portulaca, late day lilies, begonias, geraniums, crape myrtle, althea, roses, dahlias, asters, plumbago, lantana.

JULY TIPS:

- Group plants with similar water requirements.

- Before you begin gardening, rub a bar of soap over the tops of your fingernails, then dig your fingernails into it. This prevents the dirt from getting under your nails.

- If you are planning a vacation and you do not have a "plant sitter," fill your bathtub with four to six inches of water. Place empty pots upside down on a rubber mat in the water. Set your plants on top of the pots. (Use the rubber mat to keep from damaging the tub.) Tape a large piece of clear plastic over the tub. Open the curtains at the window to let in as much daylight as possible. You and your plants will enjoy the vacation for as long as three weeks.

- Continue your garden "housekeeping" by removing fading and dead flower heads.

Who loves a garden still his Eden keeps, Perennial pleasures plants, and wholesale harvest reaps.

— Bronson Alcott

July

Orchids go through a summer slump. Check to see if any need repotting. Use orchid fiber or sterilized broken redwood or pine bark. Be sure to clean the pots thoroughly and disinfect with a chlorine bleach solution.

- Don't forget that hanging planters dry out quickly. They love a good gentle shower with the hose regularly.

- Check plants for infestations of insects—aphids, cut worms, and snails—and diseases like sooty mold mildew which attacks plants when it's so humid.

- If you would like to develop a new bed or correct a bad weed situation, you can solarize the weeds away. Just put sheet of clear plastic over the area that you want weed-free and weigh down the edges. Let it sit for a few months in the hot sun. Also see "lasagna" gardening in the soil section of this book.

- July 10 is the last day to fertilize centipede grass.

- Increase watering time, but decrease frequency.

- MULCH, WATER, AND MULCH again.

MOST BUGS ARE GOOD...

Ladybugs, frogs, spiders, wasps, birds and even snakes are friends of the garden.

Marigolds attract overflies which feed on aphids.

Ants may mess up roots of plants but they benefit the garden by preying on other insects.

Spray a mixture of water and sugar on white flies. It dries them out.

Parasidic wasps fight scale insects.

August: Take care of yourself and you'll enjoy gardening more. Always use sunscreen and a hat when working in sunny yards. Drink plenty of water on hot summer days. Insect repellent is good to have with your gardening tools. Water is the focus this month – yourself and plants.

PLANT:

- Celosia, marigolds, petunias and zinnias for fall.

- Dig, divide and replant overcrowded iris, canna, day lily and spider lily.

- **Biennials:** Sow seeds now of hollyhock, wallflower, foxglove, sweet William, honesty, myosotis, and Iceland poppies. Sow directly into a well-prepared bed or a flat for transplanting.

PRUNE:

- Prune trees and shrubs lightly for cosmetic purposes.

- Check crape myrtle for powdery mildew.

- Continue to deadhead flowers as needed.

- Prune large rose bushes for heavier fall flower production.

- Stop pinching chrysanthemums so the flower buds can begin to form. To keep mums in good condition, fertilize with 1/2 lb. of 5-10-10 per 100 square feet of bed.

- Cut back petunias severely if they have gotten leggy. This will insure sturdy new growth and flowers for the fall.

The most noteworthy thing about gardeners is that they are always optimistic, always enterprising and never satisfied.

– Vita Sackville-West

August

FERTILIZE:

- Fertilize roses early this month for a fall show.

- Addition of nitrogen to the compost pile may be needed to aid decomposing of lawn clippings. Also add water during extended dry periods.

BLOOMING:

- Zinnia, salvia, aster, ginger lily, day lily, dahlias, roses and many perennials and annuals.

AUGUST TIPS:

- Deep watering for a long time is better than daily shallow watering. Be careful that plants have some water if you go on vacation.

- Water camellias, azaleas, rhododendrons for next year's blooms.

- Don't over water geraniums. They like the dry side.

- Containers: If your potted plants get so dry that the soil has shrunk or hardened, just watering the surface won't be effective. Put several inches of water in the bottom of a bucket; then set the entire pot in the water, and let dry soil soak up the moisture. After an hour remove the pot, and drain.

- Don't mow the lawn when it is under heat or drought stress.

There is no season such delight can bring,
As summer, autumn, winter and the spring.

– William Browne

September brings relief from the intense heat of summer. The air is scented with tea olive, roses, and ginger lilies...outdoor life is worth living again! Perennials may be divided and new ones planted. It is time to prepare beds for spring-flowering bulbs by working in 20% super phosphate. Enjoy your fall garden as you consider which spring-flowering bulbs to purchase this month. P.S. Take soil sample to the county extension service office to see if lime is indicated.

PLANT:
- Plant mums for fall color and lightly fertilize every two weeks.

- Survey yard for trees and shrubs that have not done well or are overgrown. Replace or transplant.

- Many wildflowers or native shrubs can be sown from seed now.

- Iris (flags): dig, divide, replant.

- Perennials may be divided and new perennials planted.

PRUNE:
- Check trees and shrubs for diseased and damaged limbs. Remove any dead or diseased wood.

FERTILIZE:
- Roses until Sept. 15

- Fertilize mums lightly, weekly until color shows, then every 2 weeks.

- Apply iron (ironite or iron sulfate) to azaleas for green leaves.

BLOOMING:
- Chrysanthemums, dahlias, marigolds, repeat day lilies, wild clematis, ageratum and asters

Morning glory at my window satisfies me more than the metaphysics of books.
— Walt Whitman

September

LAWN:
- Apply broadleaf weedkiller if necessary. Check for fungus diseases (brown patch). Treat with Terraclor. Overseed the yard for a green winter lawn if you must, but this is not very healthy in the long run. Keep moist! Mow regularly.

SEPTEMBER TIPS:
- Rake up pine straw and keep clean to use for mulch later.

- Groom container plants you intend to winter-over indoors. Repot now if roots are hanging out of the bottom of the pot. Protect newly potted plants from the sun and drying winds. Do not wait too long to take plants indoors; that artificial heat can be an awful shock to them.

- Hardy Ageratum: This wildflower makes itself comfortable in Southern gardens. It spreads by underground runners and re-seeds prolifically. Although ageratum brings a welcome spot of color, you would be wise to cut it back after the flowers fade so seeds have no chance to mature.

I smelt the violets in her hand and asked,
half in words, and half in signs, a question which meant,
"Is love the sweetness of flowers?"

— Helen Keller

October in the South is crisp with excitement; pumpkins to be carved, pansies to be planted, the State Fair to be taken in. Earthy fragrances of loquat and sasanqua mingle with tea olive and the last roses of fall. Revel in this prime gardening time. There is work to be done and the weather is perfect!

PLANT:

- Prime planting time for cool season lawns. If desired, seed lawns with annual ryegrass for winter green. Use 5 lbs. of seed per 1000 sq. ft. of lawn. Sow half the seed in one direction (east-west) and the rest in the other direction (north-south). But be aware that many experts discourage reseeding because it can be unhealthy for the lawn.

- Plant spring-flowering bulbs except for tulips. Refrigerate tulip bulbs at least 6-8 weeks before planting, in a ventilated bag. Do not put in the vegetable bin.

- Sprinkle one teaspoon slow-release fertilizer around pansies.

- Plant container, balled and burlapped trees and shrubs. Transplant shrubs, making sure to keep moist.

- Plant Lenten Roses (hellebores) now for blooms in February.

- Dig up tender summer bulbs such as caladiums, dahlias, gladiolus and elephant ear. Dry for a week and then store in peat moss for the winter, in basement or garage.

- *Flowers:* Sow seeds of poppies, larkspur, johnny-jump-up, sweet peas, forget-me-nots, and wallflowers. Scatter seeds over a well-prepared bed and rake to cover lightly. You should see seedlings this fall. They will over winter and make vigorous plants in the spring.

October gave a party;
The leaves by hundreds came;
The ashes oaks, and maples,
And those of every name.

— George Cooper

October

PRUNE:
- Do not prune hedges. It may encourage new growth.
- Continue scouting the garden for signs of diseases.
- After roses have been deadheaded and foliage has dropped, rake and dispose of all mulch and plant matter to prevent carry-over of any diseases.

FERTILIZE:
- Fertilize camellias and azaleas with 0-14-14 by mid-October to harden off plants for winter. (Since it contains no nitrogen, the fertilizer does not encourage any new growth, which could freeze.)

BLOOMING:
- Chrysanthemum, fall crocus, sasanqua, rose, marigold, zinnia, loquat, tea olive.

OCTOBER TIPS:
- **Vines:** Don't hesitate to tie uncooperative vines in place with twine or twist ties (panty hose work well). This will help your clematis, silver lace vine, climbing hydrangea, and Confederate jasmine find their way across arbors. Climbing roses will also benefit from your guidance.

- Watch for the first frost. In the midlands, the average date for the earliest frost is October 16.

- Fallen plant material like leaves and pine straw should continue to contribute to compost.

- Take your houseplants outdoors while the weather is still warm and conduct a grooming session. Repot if necessary. Check the plants for pests before bringing them back indoors.

Autumn is a second spring when every leaf's a flower.
– Albert Camus

November: Now is the ideal time to PLANT...PLANT...PLANT! From now until the end of February is the very best time of the year for almost every plant: trees, shrubs, perennials, winter annuals and bulbs. Our first frost occurs toward the first of November, so be prepared to protect.

PLANT:

- Plant evergreens, spring-flowering trees and shrubs.

- Finish planting winter annuals such as pansies, snapdragons, calendulas and candytuft, decorative cabbage and kale.

- Plant spring-flowering bulbs especially lily bulbs.

- Put tulips in the refrigerator to cool for planting in late December or early January, but not in the crisper.

PRUNE:

- Avoid pruning, which stimulates new growth (which will be killed by the frost and damage the plant). You also have to live with the "sticks" that are left until bud-break in the spring.

- Prune dead or dying foliage.

- Cut back mums after they have finished blooming to a few inches above the ground.

- Later this month, cut roses back to 3 feet.

- Avoid cutting perennials and ornamental grasses to the ground. Stems left standing help insulate the plant. Especially do not cut back lantana or verbena. They have hollow stems which can collect rain and breed disease.

- Pinch off the tips of snapdragons so they won't grow leggy.

A garden is a thing of beauty and a job forever.

NOVEMBER TIPS:

- Watch for the unexpected hard frost

- Tropical plants such as orchids, hibiscus and philodendrons should be brought indoors before the first frost.

- Potted plants, even plants that normally can survive cold nights, also should be brought in. Because of the size of the pot and the lack of insulation for roots, only the most cold-hardy plants will survive cold spells in a pot.

- Using water or sprinkler systems to protect plants from freezing temperatures is seldom practical for the homeowner. It works only when the temperature is within a few degrees of freezing, and it doesn't work on woody plants that are prone to break under the weight of the ice that forms.

- Coverings, such as plastic or mulch offer a few degrees of protection. The covering should be removed in the morning because too much heat can build up during the day and "cook" the plant.

- Clean out beds. Remove all the old mulch if it has been down more than a year. Ideally, mulch becomes part of the soil in this amount of time.

- When selecting spring-flowering bulbs remember, bigger bulb = bigger bloom.

- Gather seeds.

- If weather is dry, apply mulch to prevent the soil from freezing during occasional periods of severe cold weather.

- Lawn mower, trimmer and other mechanical tools should be cleaned and oiled before winter storage.

Half the interest of a garden is in the constant exercise of the imagination.

— Mrs. C. W. Earle

- Move potted water garden plants to deeper water to prevent freezing.

- Keep bird feeders generously filled with clean water.

- Clean up time! Pull up annuals as they finish blooming.

- Sow spring annual seeds like poppies, larspur and sweet peas in a sunny spot, now. Then about February 1, thin them. Plant them in the same area, and in a few years they should re-seed themselves.

- Average date of first frost: October 30-November 30, but it could be as early as the 2nd week of October in the midlands of SC.

- Mulch azaleas and camellias with oak leaves, pine straw, or peat moss to a depth of 3 to 4 inches. Remember not to pile mulch against the trunk.

- Divide summer-blooming perennials: daylilies, liriope, hosta.

- Cut old growth from perennials when new growth appears at the crown or when plant is totally spent. Mark where plants are if they lose all top growth during the winter. By doing this you won't plant on top of them.

- ***Sasanqua:*** Buy fall-blooming camellias now to get the color you want. The flowers of sasanqua camellia are smaller but similar to those of the common camellia. Sasanqua have essentially the same cultural requirements as azaleas — acid soil, good drainage, and partial shade.

November

FERTILIZE:

- Give bulbs "bulb booster" fertilizer (5-10-20) because bulbs are growing roots. If you are planting new bulbs, mix fertilizer into the bed. Putting fertilizer into the hole may burn the roots.

- Keep lawn free of leaves and straw. Apply a fall formulation such as 20-9-9 where available.

- Spray camellias and azaleas with dormant oil spray to protect against scale. Follow directions on bottle paying particular attention to temperature range.

BLOOMING:

- Chrysanthemums, early camellias, holly, pyracantha and nandina

*Gather ye rosebuds while ye may,
Old time is still a-flying:
And this same flower that smiles today,
tomorrow will be dying.*

– Robert Herrick

Forcing Paper-Whites

Choose any container that will hold water. A taller container may help to support the stems so that they will not fall over. Add a thin layer of small rocks, pebbles, marbles, or soil. Clean the bulbs of any loose brown skin and place them, roots down, point up, on the pebbles then add more pebbles until only the noses of the bulbs are showing (when the roots form, they will push the bulbs upward). Add enough water to wet the round flat area on the bottom of the bulb. When roots form, the water level should be allowed to drop until only the roots are wet and the bulb is high and dry. When the leaves appear, try to give the bulbs as much sun as possible and to keep them as cool as possible.

Paper-whites can be potted in potting soil. Any well-draining soil will do but the container will need drainage holes. If your paper-whites tend to fall over, try giving the bulbs more light and less heat. To stake them, tie the leaves together with a raffia bow and add a branch with many twigs (azaleas work well) in the middle.

The average time from first green leaves to flowers is approximately 21 days. Flowering can be hastened a little by moving the container to a warmer, bright place and slowed somewhat by moving the container to a cooler, dark place. To enjoy blooms over a season, start a new set of bulbs every two weeks or so.

*I used to love my garden, but now my love is dead;
I found Bachelor's Button in Black-eyed Susan's Bed.*

– Seen at Brookgreen Garden

Perennials

Annuals die after one season; biennials last 2 years; but perennials last for many years and get bigger so you can divide them and create many baby plants. Sound too good to be true? Well, yes, there are negatives – perennials often have a short blooming season and some grow so thick that they must be divided to continue blooming. As the joke goes, " a perennial is a plant that if it had lived, would have come back year after year." But if you plan carefully, perennials can add much to your garden.

Perennials look wonderful in a mixed garden, especially with shrubs for definition, and annuals to provide long-lived blooms. Perennials usually don't bloom too long, so you need to plan for the foliage. Because perennials are long-lived, the time to improve the soil and add irrigation is before you plant. Generally soaker hoses are better than overhead sprays, but some kind of irrigation system is a must in the Midlands. Because of space and the difficulty of classification we have included some bulbs, ground covers and vines.

PERENNIAL HINTS:
- Hand pull weeds to avoid damaging shallow roots.

- Many newly-planted perennials will not bloom the first year. Some even take a few years.

- Remove dead foliage and stems in the fall. Mulch to protect crowns and roots from alternating mild and freezing weather and dry spells.

- Many perennials should be staked to prevent them from bending or falling over. When staking is done correctly, the plants will grow to cover the stakes. Azalea sticks work well. Asters need a grid and lilies need a loop kind of support.

- Remove old flowers to encourage re-bloom, which is called dead-heading. Many should be cut back to ground level after blooming has finished to encourage new leaf growth from the base. Usually wait to cut back after leaves have turned brown.

- Many perennials grow into such thick clumps that performance declines because the plants are too crowded. When this happens, dig up the clump during its dormant period and divide it.

SOME FAVORITE PERENNIALS:

Iris: Irises come in many shapes, colors and blooming characteristics. All types will bloom best in full sun, but soil, moisture and climatic requirements vary with each type. By selecting from the bearded, beardless and bulbous varieties you can stretch the iris season well past May and June. The tiny bulbous iris, danfordiae and reticulata, begin the show in early March. Bearded iris bloom from late April until the middle of June, but each plant usually only blooms for a few weeks. Dwarf bearded iris blooms arrive in May. Many of these have the extra bonus of being fragrant. The Siberian iris and Japanese iris will be the late bloomers of the family.

Black-eyed Susan (Rudbeckia): Black-eyed Susans are long living and easy to grow. They bloom from July to September and will last and last when cut. Plant in sun to part shade.

Carolina Jessamine: Everyone needs to have the S.C. state flower. This perennial vine blooms in the early spring and has a wonderful fragrance. It grows in any kind of soil and does fine in shade but flowers better in the sun. It grows 1 to 2 feet per year (careful, it could become invasive). Baby plants will pop up from seeds all around the mother plant.
It does need support, like a tree to grow onto.

If you have a garden and a library you have everything you need.
— Cicero

Chrysanthemum or garden mum is perhaps best known for its fall flowers. Some have handsome variegated leaves which are an asset to the garden all year long. When you buy mums in pots, look for ones with buds that are closed or just starting to open. Put them in the ground where the roots stay moist and they'll bloom for a longer period than if they are kept in pots. During the year keep them pinched back for bushier plants. Propagate by cuttings or division of old plants in the early spring. Plants should be divided after three years. "Ryan's or Becky's Daisy" has shasta-type blooms, strong 18" stems and is a great flower.

HINTS FOR MUMS:

- Proper care and pinching off new growth in the spring and midsummer can coax mums to bloom twice – fall and spring – and help the plant keep a compact shape.

- Be sure you are not buying florist's mums, which are great plants for an indoor table setting, but they will not do well if you want to plant them outdoors in the garden. Instead, buy hardy mums, which are bred to survive cooler weather.

- Find a well-drained sunny site in your garden. Mums will not do well in shade or in soggy sites.

- Mix several shovels full of compost into the ground where you plant your mums. The compost helps create good drainage and gives the mum's roots an extra boost to spread out and dig in.

- Plant in large numbers and drifts.

Hosta (Plantain Lily): Hosta does best in light shade but can tolerate sun and full shade. It prefers moist soil enriched with compost of leaf mold. Propagate by dividing clumps in early spring, but it will do fine without any division. They seem to disappear in the winter, so be careful not to dig them up. Hostas collapse to nothing in the winter, but oh, they do put on a long leafy show the rest of the year. They are easy to grow and to propagate by division. They come in ever increasing varieties of sizes, leaf textures, colors and variegations. They appreciate fertilizer once a year. They are good in containers. But they can have problems with slugs.

Angel's Trumpet (Brugmansia): Fabulous in bloom, it is easy to grow, but hard to classify. In mid S.C. it looks like it is dead in the winter but does come back in late spring and blooms beautifully in late summer to fall. It grows very large, small tree size, from its stunted growth in just one season. Try and shield it from damaging wind. Expect frost damage and unattractive winter appearance. Prune in early Spring. The cut stems can be easily propagated in water. You may grow in pots and move to your basement in the winter. Do make sure there is a large hole for drainage. Once they start budding they grow very fast so they require a lot of water and a lot of fertilizer (bloom buster like 10-50-10.) The flowers are trumpet-shaped but lean down, so if they are in a pot, it is nice to elevate them on a table to really enjoy the blooms. The flowers are very fragrant and are offered in many beautiful colors: white, pink, orange, yellow.

The best place to find God is in a garden.
You can dig for Him there.

– George Bernard Shaw

Ferns are wonderful evergreen additions to gardens. Many are hardy perennials in South Carolina. They are generally grown best in rich soil (do not add lime) in shady areas. Ferns thrive with light applications of organic fertilizer in spring and late summer. But some are sensitive to chemical fertilizer. Ferns are propagated by spores which are on the under side of the fronds. Do mulch them with about 3 inches of bark mulch. It is not necessary to cut old debris out. It is important to water ferns frequently in hot, dry weather.

- **Holly fern:** wonderfully evergreen from the coast up to the mountains, where it is deciduous.
- **Ebony Spleenwort:** low growing, 6 inches in poor soil.
- **Cinnamon fern:** can grow to 6 feet in rich soil, young fronds are called fiddleheads.
- **Japanese Painted fern:** beautiful accent, grows to 16 inches, slow spreading clump.
- **Boston fern:** frost-tender, consider it a house plant except at the coast.
- **Ostrich fern:** tolerates some sun if has adequate water, dormant in winter, best in upper state. Can grow to 6 feet.
- **Lady ferns:** can grow to 4 feet, vigorous, can tolerate more sun in moist soil.
- **Shield fern:** 6-18 inches, shaggy yellowish green.
- **Autumn fern:** erect growth to 2 feet, color changes throughout year, tolerates some drought.
- **Christmas fern:** easy to grow, evergreen, grows about 14 inches, stiff upright.
- **Wood fern (SouthernShield):** can grow to 3 feet, vigorous, tolerates limey drier soil and more sun than other ferns.

But though an old man, I am but a young gardener.

– Thomas Jefferson

Ornamental grasses are being used more in our gardens for good reasons. They tolerate a wide variety of soils and temperatures and are nearly insect and disease free. In the fall when other perennials are pooped out, they are playfully waving their colorful plums in the breeze. They can be diminutive and delicate for the tiny courtyard to invasive giants for large estates. The dead foliage can be attractive in winter then cut back in early spring. Multiply by division. The list below all grow best in full sun.

	HEIGHT	**SPREAD**
Japanese Sweet Flag	6-12 in.	6 in.
Will tolerate part shade, moist areas		
Pampass Grass	8-10 ft.	5-6 ft.
Giant plumes, difficult to control		
Dwarf Pampass	3-4 ft	3-4 ft.
More manageable		
Miscanthus	5-6 ft.	3-4 ft.
Prominent white midrift. Popular varieties: Japanese silver, maiden, zebra.		
Switch Grass	5 ft.	4 ft.
Moist site, good in arrangements		
Rose Fountain	16 in.	2 ft.
Almost black spikes		
Fountain Grass	4 ft.	3 ft.
Sensitive May be an annual		

Day lily (Hemerocallis): These are ideal plants for sunny gardens. They require little care. They are not known for diseases and will flourish in any soil. They don't require dividing, spraying or special fertilizers. They come in most all of the colors. The only problem can be guessed by their name: the blooms usually only last a day. Thus they are not good for flower arrangements, but all things considered, they are exceptional plants.

A good Daylily year:

- **March** - Plant seeds for hybridizing in pots that have been kept in the refrigerator.
- **April** - Apply 10-10-10 fertilizer, when foliage appears.
- **May** - Give the ladybugs and praying mantises a chance to control pests such as aphids, thrips, and spider mites. If an infestation threatens to get out of control, apply Disyston, a granular systemic. Apply Osmocote (slow release fertilizer) when the weather warms. Remember to water, especially as the lilies first come up.
- **June** - Enjoy the blooms. Watch for spider mites, especially in dry years. Set out beer traps for slugs or use Epsom salts. Dead-head spent blooms.
- **July** - Still blooming. Continue dead heading. Pull off leaves with leaf streaks. Spray every two weeks with fungicide, as needed.
- **August** - More blooms. Still dead-heading.
- **September** - Divide and move large clumps late in the month. Look out for plant sales and swaps.
- **October** - Prepare new beds. Continue dividing.
- **November** - Some varieties may be still blooming! Clean up beds after the first frost.
- **December/January/February** - Plan new day lilies to try.

PERENNIALS THAT TOLERATE MOIST OR DAMP SOILS:		
aster	confederate rose	royal fern
elephant's ear	Japanese iris	forget me not
sweet woodruff	blue lobia	calla
astilbe	cardinal flower	day lily
canna	bee balm	swamp sunflower

PERENNIALS FOR HOT, DRY CONDITIONS (SUN):

yarrow	perennial sunflower	coneflower
century plant	yucca	sedum
artemesia	goldenrod	verbena
false indigo	hens & chickens	phlox
coreopsis	bearded iris	mums
butterfly weed	red hot poker	daisy
guara	lamb's ear	pink dianthus
lantana	Mexican petunia	Provence lavender
pampass grass	Mexican sage	salvia (sage)
day lily	canna	petunias
Russian sage	rudbeckia	(old-fashioned ones)
	veronica	

EASY TO GROW. OH, YES, CAREFUL... THEY ARE INVASIVE!
CAREFUL IF JUNGLE OR SWAMP IS IN ITS NAME

yarrow	Chinese wisteria	wild ageratum
elaeagnus	chinaberry	spiderwort
privet, ligustrum	princess tree	yellow loosestrife
honeysuckle	mimosa tree	Chinese tallow tree
nandina	mexican petunia	(popcorn)
English ivy	obedient plant	tawny day lily (old type
vinca	mints	orange flowers)
bamboo	trumpet vine	

PERENNIALS FOR SHADE:

hardy cyclamen	hosta	ajuga
primrose	crested iris	anemone
astilbe	cardinal flower	lady's mantle
cast iron plant	blue lobelia	wild blue phlox
ferns(most)	bluebells	foxglove (reseeds)
lenten rose	lily of the valley	creeping woodland
hardy begonia	forget me not	phlox

Tropicals are those lush jungle-looking plants. Many have gigantic leaves and come in all colors from near black to neon lime. Some tropicals are hardy but some must be protected from winter freezes.

Tips:

- Most thrive in heat and humidity.

- Most thrive with abundant water and fertilizer during growing periods, BUT not when dormant or indoors.

- The bigger and greener the plant, the more it will appreciate nitrogen (first number on fertilizer label).

- Flowering plants need more phosphorus (the middle number on fertilizer label).

- Move tender plants inside before first frost (about October in SC). Keep them in pots. Return outside after the last frost (about April).

- Indoors: Place the plants in the same general lighting environment they enjoyed outside. Withhold fertilizer and only lightly water inside.

- When returning plants outdoors, protect them from direct sunlight at first. Slowly acclimate them by first placing them in shade for a few days.

- Consider the length of the freeze. It is usually only a concern if it lasts more than a few hours.

Some wonderful "annual tropicals" can be protected inside in winter, then enjoyed and multiplied in the spring, like begonias and coleus, which are easy to root in water.

Sometimes it is easier to store only the bulb instead of the whole plant. Dig up the plant from the garden before the first freeze and cut the leaves away. Store the bulbs (or corns) in saw dust. Do not water at all. They'll be fine protected from freezing in areas like a garage or basement. Some of these plants include caladiums, ornamental sweet potato vine, and tender elephant ears (like Alocasia sanderiana).

Some tropicals are hardy outside. Before the first frost, cut them down and heavily mulch. Remove the mulch in spring. Be careful that roots do not freeze. Potted plants may need extra protection. Gingers, lobster claw, bananas, crinums, spider lily, hibiscus, red amaryllis, many elephant ears need heavy mulch outside.

The Earth laughs in flowers.

— Ralph Waldo Emerson

Annuals

Annuals are like beautiful accessories in the garden. They add sparkle to any garden, offering continuous blooms over a long period and an almost boundless variety of colors, shapes, and sizes. They die after only one season, having bloomed proficiently, then give you the chance to try something new next year. There are two main categories of annuals. Warm-season annuals which bloom when there is no frost and the days and nights are warm (& even hot). Some favorites are impatiens and petunias. Cool-season annuals do tolerate frost but do not tolerate heat. Winter would not be the same without pansies.

WHERE TO PLANT:
- Best when planted in a carefully prepared bed (double digging is best), in well-drained soil (may need to add peat moss and organic material), and with plenty of sun and sufficient water.

- A few annuals will tolerate moderate shade, but most will not grow well in dense shade, except impatiens and coleus.

WHEN TO PLANT:
- **For warm-season annuals:** early Spring, after the last frost, which in Columbia is usually mid-April.
- **For cool-season annuals:** late Summer or Autumn.

HOW TO PLANT ANNUALS:
Annual seeds offer many varieties, but more patience to grow. Some seeds to try by sowing directly where you want them to grow are nasturtium, cleome, zinnia, and cosmos. Some cool-season annual seeds to try are larkspur and poppies. Transplants in flats are great for that instant garden, and so much fun to pick out in early spring. Your local farmers' market will have good selections. To hasten growth and blooms, warm-season annuals need to establish roots before hot (and usually dry) days. Set out cool-season annuals while days are still warm enough for good plant growth.

Any weed that goes to seed - Next year you'll regret the deed.

Many annuals re-seed. Try planting seeds (poppies, larkspur, sweet peas) in the same location for a few years. In early February thin out the smallest plants so that you will have strong plants left.

WATERING:
When watering, hold the hose nozzle down near the base of the plants and gently, but thoroughly soak the soil. Drip irrigation is usually better than overhead spraying. Don't forget to mulch, it conserves soil moisture and keeps down weeds. Many annuals sold at garden centers are water junkies because they receive so much water and fertilizer. Break this habit by trimming them back 1/3 before planting. This also helps prevent them from becoming leggy.

FERTILIZING:
Mix a slow-release complete fertilizer into the soil before planting annuals. This generally supplies enough nutrients to last several months. In about 6 weeks use a bloom- booster fertilizer, such as 15-30-15 or 15-40-15. Continue to feed with liquid fertilizer.

DEAD-HEADING:
To keep blooms all season long, remove spent blossoms before the plant can begin seed formation. This channels the plants energy towards producing more flowers instead of seeds. Usually cut or pinch back to the next bud below the spent bloom.

COOL-SEASON SUN ANNUALS		
Kale	Cabbage	Alyssum
Mustard	Pansies	Petunias
Stock	Dianthus	Snapdragons
	Violas	

WARM-SEASON ANNUALS FOR THE SHADE

These annuals tolerate the light shade under the high limbs of big trees or under pines.

Caladium	Forget-me-Not	Coleus
Penta	Begonias	Foxglove
Black-eyed Susan Vine	Scarlet Sage	Flowering tobacco
Cleome	Wishbone Flower	Impatiens

ANNUALS FOR HOT SUMMERS

These do well despite a late start, even in S.C. heat.

Vinca	Sunflower	Salvia
Gomphrena Pentas	Hyacinth bean	Dusty Miller
Sun Coleus	Hibiscus	Madagascar periwinkle
Impatiens	Portulaca	Verbena
Moonflower	Bachelor Button	Castor bean
Begonia	Cockscomb	Gloriosa daisy
Marigolds	Datura	Mexican Oregano
Zinnia	Morning-Glory	Dahlia
Caladium	Petunias	Scaevola 'Blue Wonder'

LONG BLOOMING ANNUALS

Annuals that you can set out right after the last frost in Spring and that will last until the first frost of Fall. They will continue to bloom without deadheading.

Impatiens	Lantana
New Guinea Impatiens	Moonflower
Begonia	Gomphrenao
Blue ageratum	Pentas
Morning-Glory	Coleus
Narrow-leaf Zinnia	Petunia

What sunshine is to flowers, smiles are to humanity.

SOME FAVORITE ANNUALS

- **Ageratum-dwarf:** good for borders.
- **Begonia:** partial sun, avoid afternoon sun. DragonWing gets huge and takes more sun.
- **Candytuft:** good for augmenting perennial candytuft.
- **Cleome:** this re-seeds and blooms until-big.
- **Coleus:** good shape and colors. Many sizes, needs drainage, new varieties are more sun-tolerant.
- **Cosmos:** easy and good cutting plants. Very tall cornflowers.
- **Dahlias:** easy from seed, dwarf are particularly good.
- **Impatiens:** shade, needs moisture, plant in masses.
- **Gaillardia:** very easy.
- **Hollyhock:** grows tall.
- **Dusty Miller:** partial to full sun, silvery foliage.
- **Larkspur:** very easy and re-seeds itself.
- **Marigolds:** full sun.
- **Moonflower Vine:** beautiful & fragrant at night.
- **Nasturtium:** very easy – sow in winter.
- **Periwinkle:** easy, stands drought and heat
- **Pansies:** full to partial sun, likes cool seasons, not summer.
- **Petunias:** Partial to full sun. Wave type is vigorous.
- **Poppies**
- **Rudbeckia:** gloriosa daisies, re-seeds.
- **Coneflowers**
- **Salvia:** partial to full sun – remember to dead-head.
- **Snapdragons:** partial to full sun.
- **Tithonial:** needs space, wonderful for cut flowers.
- **Sweet Alyssum:** partial to full sun, low-growing.
- **Sweet William:** foliage first year, flowers the second. Root stems in soil.
- **Viola:** wonderful border plant.
- **Zinnia:** full sun, good cut flowers.

RARE, THREATENED AND ENDANGERED PLANTS

Garden Club of South Carolina, Inc., 1989 (June 2003)

Many plants native to our state are becoming rare and in danger of extinction. The Garden Club of South Carolina urges everyone to refrain from picking or digging these endangered species. Members are prohibited from using them in any exhibit.

Black- Spored Quillwort
Bunched Arrowhead
Canby's Dropwort
Chaffseed
Dwarf-Flowered Heartleaf
Harperella
Miccosukee Gooseberry
Michaux's Sumac
Mountain Sweet Pitcher
Persistent Trillium
Pondberry

Pool Sprite
Reflexed Blue-Eyed Grass
Relict Trillium
Rocky Gnome Lichen
Rough-Leaved Loosestrife
Schweinitz's Sunflower
Seabeach Amaranth
Small Whorled Pogonia
Smooth Coneflower
Swamp-Pink

The Garden Club of South Carolina, Inc., recommends support of the **Heritage Trust Conservation** list. This list may be obtained free from:

Heritage Trust Section
S.C. Department of Natural Resources
P.O. Box 167
Columbia, S.C. 29202

(803) 734-3894

*If of this plant you don't see many,
then be a good guy and don't pick any!*

RBOR DAY

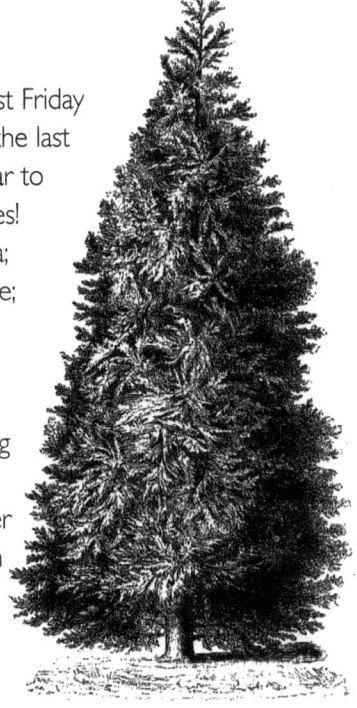

Arbor Day in South Carolina is the first Friday in December. National Arbor Day is the last Friday in April. It is an ideal time of year to plant in our area, so join in the activities! Plant one or more trees in a civic area; establish a systematic plan for tree care; make a display of trees; or learn more about trees.

Arbor Day is set aside for tree planting in many towns in America and several foreign countries. It was launched over a century ago by J. Sterling Morton, an editor and political leader, as a local newspaper campaign to plant trees on Nebraska's treeless prairies. Morton moved to Nebraska in 1822 with memories of the lush landscape of his Michigan home. Today his home-place, now a park called Arbor Lodge, displays 150 different varieties of trees and shrubs. His son, Joy, continued his enthusiasm for tree planting and founded the 1,500 acre Morton Arboretum in 1992 at Lisle, Illinois, where 4,800 different types of plants are cultivated.

Show your concern for the future by planning a special Arbor Day celebration. Insure that your children and grandchildren will know the beauty and usefulness of tress.

For information, log on to www.arborday.org

Trees

South Carolina has a great variety of trees. We can grow exotic tropical palms and mountainous cool looking evergreens. Like with plants, you must be careful that the tree is planted in the proper conditions. Trees are usually longer lived and much larger than plants and shrubs, so the site location is very important.

PLANTING TIPS:

- Before you dig, call 1-800-922-0983 for underground utilities.

- Generally it is best to plant in the fall (November through mid-March) so the tree can prepare for winter cold, spring blooming, and summer heat.

- Dig hole twice as wide as root ball and one and one-half times as deep (then refill some soil). Be careful not to plant too deep, root ball should be slightly above ground.

- Fill dirt around tree loosely, create a mound around edge to create a watering saucer.

- Mulch heavily around the base, at least as wide as the root ball. But do not get the mulch up against the bark or it will promote rot and disease in the tree.

- Add slow release fertilizer, may need to repeat application for a few years.

- Do not apply high nitrogen fertilizer at planting because it may burn tender roots.

- Remove burlap from top third of the root ball. If the tree has guide wires or stakes, remove them after the first year.

- Water well for the first week, then continue to monitor water for first few years.

- Do not "top off" trees, it's bad for their health. If in doubt call a specialist.

- Do not mutilate crape myrtles, trimming is OK but do not butcher.

- Dogwoods in mid-Carolina should not be in complete sun. Do be careful to water. Even well-established Dogwoods have been killed during our recent summer droughts. Do not transplant from woods. Dogwoods like good drainage and not heavily packed soil. Slow growers.

The City of Columbia Forestry Division, (803)733-8457, has a great pamphlet *"City Trees"* which has a community tree selection list. Sterling Garden Center has *"City Trees"* at their counter.

CITRUS TREES

Yes, we can grow **citrus trees** in South Carolina. Citrus trees like good drainage and sandy soil. They do not like soggy feet. Do protect them from cold winds by placing them on the south side of a fence or house. Flowers tend to bloom around Easter and the fruits are ready for picking around thanksgiving. They do well in containers, which are nice to be able to bring indoors during cold spells.

COLD-HARDY CITRUS FOR SOUTH CAROLINA:

Bitter Lemon Kumquat	Juanita tangerine
Changsha mandarin	Sanbokan grapefruit
Citrandarin	Satsuma mandarin
Citrumelo	10-degree tangerine
Ichang Lemon	Thomasville citrangequat

I think I shall never see, A poem as lovely as a tree.
A tree that may in summer wear, A nest of robins in her hair.
Upon whose bosom snow has lain,
Who intimately lives with rain.

— Alfred Joyce Kilmer

GOOD LAWN SHADE TREES

(yes, you should be able to grow grass under these).
- **Male Gingko Maiden Tree** – Produces no fruit. Full sun, heat tolerant.
- **Pine Trees** – Yes, Pines have many fine qualities, Use them, You probably already have some.
- **Sabal Palmetto** – So State Capital looking.
- **White Oak** – Large majestic tree with white bark.
- **Pin Oaks** – Pyramid shape, takes full sun and adapts to many sites.
- **American Beech** – Needs well drained, loose soil.
- **Bald Cypress** – Withstands poor drainage.
- **Tulip Poplar** – Likes full sun, needs loose, moist soil and space to develop.

SMALL TREES

- **Winter-flowering Cherry** – Fast-growing to 15 feet, twiggy and tight canopy with pink or white flowers covering the tree in February.
- **Japanese Maple** – Partial shade, provides spring & fall color; "Blood good" has a reddish purple leaf color.
- **Redbuds** – Try Cercis canadensis selections ("Flame" is a great one). Profuse lavender blooms; turns yellow-green in the fall. A good patio, lawn or street tree.
- **Magnolia " Little Gem", "Kay Parris"** – are slow-growing so appear dwarf, but both eventually reach 40 feet.
- **Yaupon Holly** – adaptable evergreen has scarlet fruit.
- **Dogwood** – Needs partial shade. Slow and can be difficult to establish.

An Apple-tree puts to shame all the men and women that have attempted to dress since the world began.

– Henry Ward Beecher

TREES THAT LIKE DRY, SANDY SOIL
- **Crape-myrtle** – full sun, heat tolerant. Beautiful summer flowers.
- **Willow Oak** – good street tree, pyramidal shape.
- **Leyland Cypress** – evergreen, full sun, fast growth, good screen.
- **Honey locust, thornless** – casts light shade.

FAST GROWING TREES (as long as you water and fertilize regularly)
But be warned, fast growing can sometimes be weaker.
- **Eucalyptus** – Many species with lots of different leaf shapes available. Grows 10 feet a summer.
- **Leyland Cypress** – A fast-growing tree but also gets a lot of pest problems. Gets to 40 feet tall. It is often used improperly.
- **Cupressus arizonica "Carolina Sapphire"** – Available in large home stores. Beautiful blue conifer that will grow 3 feet a year even in dry soil. This evergreen is good for color year-round.
- **Waxmyrtle** – Quickly becomes a small tree. Grows to 25 feet. Good as a hedge.
- **Windmill Palm** – Will grow one foot a year, but is highly dependent on water and fertilizer.
- **Oriental Persimmon Tree** – Grows to 25 feet and can be as wide. They are handsome trees with large oval leaves, and delicious fruit. The best cultivars for SC are Fuyugaki and Hachiya. The fruit is ripe when it is as soft as a ripe peach.

TREES TO AVOID
- **Bradford Pear** – Trees are short-lived; they split and break up and cause property damage.
- **Female Ginkgo Maiden Trees** – Have beautiful leaves and yellow fall color, but the fruit of the female trees is mushy.
- **Crab Apples** – Some do well here but most, and many other trees that are common in the North, don't live very long in our climate.
- **Sugar Maples** – Substitute Southern Sugar Maple here in the South.
- **Magnolias** – Avoid in small places, great if carefully sited. Big leaves are hard to rake up. But there are now small varieties.
- **Sweet Gum** – prickly balls are terrible on bare feet.
- **Sycamore** – hard to clean up.
- **Wax Myrtles** – suffer during ice storms but after the dead wood is removed they will come back.

GENERAL PALM TREE HINTS

Many Palms will be damaged in cold and especially if the cold lasts a long time. Do try and protect the newly growing middle fronds, and site sensitive palms in protected areas like the south side of a brick house. But do not throw away palms that seem dead, wait until the spring and prune away most of the damage and watch the middle crown for greening up.

Make sure you locate the Palm where it can reach its full height because you can not prune the height, because its new growth occurs from the high central growing point.

Palms like sandy soil, they require good drainage; they do not like wet feet. If you have clay soil add sand, mushroom compost, gypsum, super phosphate and root simulator. If you have sandy soil then add all of the above items in the surrounding soil except sand and gypsum. Do water them when they are newly planted, but be careful, the worst thing to do is to over water. Water once a day for the first week after planting. Once established only water if really needed, and do not frequently lightly water, instead water thoroughly. They are best planted in spring or summer.

Palms are low maintenance plants, they do not require much pruning. But you may remove some of the brown fronds to improve its appearance. Never injure the lead newly forming frond, because the tree will die if it is injured. Generally, do not remove any fronds that are growing horizontally or pointed upward.

Excessive numbers of older yellow fronds could indicate a defiency of potassium or magnesium (and be careful not to fertilize with too high nitrogen numbers) There is special palm fertilizer.

If scale appears on the leaves of the palm, spray with Dormant Oil. For prevention of borers, spray with Diazinon4E in spring and fall.

Check the Internet:
The Southeastern Palm and Exotic Plant Society
www.speps.net

Sabal Palmetto Tree, Cabbage Palm

Sago Palm

PALM TREES

- **Sabal Palmetto Tree** – The South Carolina State Tree. A native palm tree for S.C. that grows slowly to a height of 30 feet with a spread of 10 to 15 feet. Also known as cabbage Palm.
- **Windmill Palm Trees** – A true cold hardy tree, they grow to a height of 20 feet here in South Carolina. They grow very fast, up to 2 feet per year. The Windmill have no pest problems, and will grow in poor clay soils if not over watered and properly fertilized.
- **Saw Palmetto or Scrub Palm** – A low, spreading palm, they are aggressive spreaders in coastal regions.
- **Needle Palm** – Native to the flood plains of the Southeast, they have a clumping habit and very sharp needles.
- **Mediterranean Fan Palm** – A small clumping fan palm with stiff leaves, it is a slow grower to its final height of 5 feet.
- **Washingtonia** – Can grow to 60 feet in coastal areas, but it is only hardy to 18 degrees.
- **Feather or Jelly Palm** – has long flexible arching fronds that grow to 6 to 8 feet. The tree itself grows at a slow to moderate rate to 10 to 20 feet.
- **Sago Palm** – is not a true palm but is a cycad. Can be used like a palm and makes a wonderful specimen plant. It grows to about 4 feet around and in height. It may be damaged by cold below 10 degrees, especially if it is a prolonged cold. In mid to upper South Carolina, it's fronds will freeze and turn brown. Trim them after you notice new growth in spring.

The most noteworthy thing about gardeners is that they are always optimistic, always enterprising and never satisfied.

– Vita Sackville-West

Shrubs

Surely shrubs are the backbones of the midlands garden. Shrubs do so many things from foundation plantings, to screens, to providing the green lush back ground for flower beds, to the single focal point ornament. They are generally low maintenance and live long. The only real criticism of shrubs is that we seem to use the same ones. Only about fifty kinds of shrubs make up 75 percent of all shrubs sold. And sometimes in the midlands we seem to only have azaleas & camellias.

In order for shrubs to be low maintenance you must research the mature size. If you have a bush that grows to 6 feet under your 3 foot high window, you are going to have to trim it often. So do the research before you plant.

SOME FAVORITE SHRUBS

- **Azaleas** – *Can there be too much of a good thing?* Azaleas grow from 2 to 20 feet high at maturity and about the same width. They prefer acidic soil (love pine needle mulch), regular watering, good drainage and open shade. Try to buy when they are blooming so that you can check the color (Oh, what great colors!). They enjoy light fertilization after they have bloomed. Prune after blooming, so that you will not be cutting next years buds.

- **Boxwood** – Widely used for edges, hedges, foundation plants and can be pruned into small trees. Left unclipped, they usually grow round and billowing. Grow slowly from 4 to 15 feet. Like fertile, moist soil, sun or shade and needs excellent drainage. Can be susceptible to many diseases and pests.

Love of flowers and vegetables is not enough to make a good gardener. He must also hate weeds.

– Eugene P. Bertin

- **Gardenia –** Gardenias are temperamental, but the fragrance and beautiful blooms are worth the trouble. They like acid soil, light shade, regular water and feeding, and good soil drainage. Do not disturb their roots. Several insects and diseases are likely to show up on your gardenia- but persevere.

- **Loropetalum –** These have recently become so popular because they perform year round, with show stopping blossoms in the spring of red, purple, or pink, and then evergreen leaves the rest of the year. These are informal acid-loving evergreen shrubs.

- **Tea Olive –** The tea olive could be considered a small tree. They have a heavenly fragrance. They prefer well-drained soil, sun or part shade, medium to high moisture and are generally insect and disease resistant.

SHRUBS FOR THE SHADE

Sweet shrub	sweet box
hydrangea	viburnum
nandina	eleagnus
daphne	azalea
laurel	gardenia
leatherleaf mahonia	fatsia
anise	yew
aucuba	pieris
camellia	hollies

SHRUBS FOR SUN TO PART SHADE

abelia	wintersweet	laurel
elaeagnus	boxwood	sweet olive
nandina	viburnum	pittosporum
snowball	anises	hollies
beautyberry	gardenia	loropetalum
sweetshrub	wax myrtle	indian hawthrone

Hydrangeas

It is hard to decide if hydrangeas are best enjoyed in the garden or in flower arrangements. They prefer light shade, regular water, rich soil and benefit from spring feeding. All types are hardy in Zone 7 and tolerate our hot, humid summers well. These shrubs produce gorgeous blossoms beginning in late May that range in color from deep blue, purple and violet to red, pink, and white and vary in size from 12-18 inches to 8 feet. They are all deciduous. Hydrangea blooms are shaped like globes, discs, or fat cones, which help determine how they are grouped.

The most widely known garden varieties are **bigleaf or French Hydrangeas**, H. macrophylla. Of these there are two types: hortensias (mopheads - globe shaped flower heads) and lace caps (flat disc shaped flower heads). H. macrophylla bloom on the previous year's growth and respond well to pruning after flowering. Plants that are five years old will benefit when two to three of the oldest stems are pruned out to eight inches from the ground. This tends to rejuvenate the plant. Proven cultivars are Maria Theresa, Blue Wave, and Lanarth White to name only a few of many. The bigleaf mopheads will have blue flowers in acid soil and pink blooms in alkaline soil.

A garden is a grand teacher.

— Gertrude Jekyll

H. Anomala, **climbing hydrangeas**, rarely need pruning. Take out only diseased or dead wood. Often they take several years to establish, but they are worth the wait.

Our native hydrangea, H. Quercifolia, **Oak-Leaf**, is an all-time favorite. It tolerates our heat and humidity extremely well and even thrives in full sun. Its brilliant crimson color in autumn is spectacular. Fat cone-shaped blooms (panicles) appear in mid-May and last for several weeks. Snow Queen and Snow Flake are favorite cultivars. This group should not be pruned unless it is necessary to control growth. If you must, take out no more than one third of the plant and do it immediately following flowering.

H. arborescens is our other southeastern native and also has white flower heads. They are generally known as **Grandiflora**. This group blooms on new wood (current year's growth) and can therefore be cut back severely in the very early spring. **Annabelle** and **Grandiflora** are the most well know cultivars. Some gardeners have gotten Annabelle to re-bloom if all spent flower heads are removed immediately.

H. Paniculata is named for its cone-shaped flower heads. It can be trained as a shrub, standard or tree. It blooms on new wood so it can be pruned in the early spring or just left alone. **Peegee** and **Tarrdiva** are good examples. The Peegee, in mid to late summer, has white foot-long flowers, which fade to pink. The abundance of heavy blossoms causes the branches to bend, causing a fountain of flowers. They are beautiful in the upstate and even do fine in coastal gardens.

www.hydrangea.com is worth checking out.

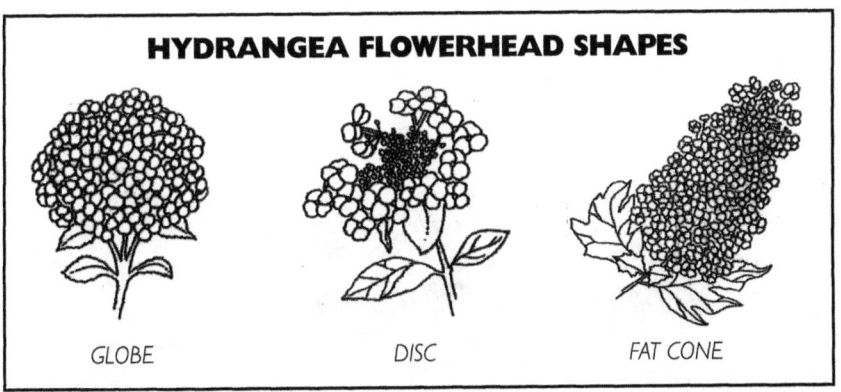

HYDRANGEA FLOWERHEAD SHAPES

GLOBE   DISC   FAT CONE

PRUNING HYDRANGEAS

Remember less is better than more when pruning hydrangeas. Avoid hard pruning. Determine when to prune by when the buds are set:

Buds on old wood, prune after blooming; if buds on new wood, prune in the very early spring.

The basic reasons to prune are to remove dead or diseased wood, or to control excessive growth. It's a good idea to leave spent flower heads through the winter as they protect the new buds until spring.

H. macrophylla	Bigleaf	prune soon after flowering
H. arborescen	Annabelle, Grandiflora	prune early spring
H. paniculata	Peegee	prune early spring, or leave alone
H. anomala	Climbing hydrangeas	do not prune
H. quercifolia	Oak-Leaf	do not prune

Hydrangeas prefer loamy, slightly acid, well-drained soil that is evenly moist with abundant organic content. They have shallow root systems so be careful around the roots. As a rule they prefer dappled-shade and one to two inches of water per week. Leaves will signal when the plant needs water. However, when the temperature reaches about 90 degrees, the leaves may wilt even if they have sufficient water. The macrophyllas are most affected by these conditions Cover the base of the plant with at least two inches of mulch. Fertilize before the leaves emerge and after blooming. This split application will help control the amount of nitrogen the plant absorbs at one time which cuts down on excessive leaf growth. Use fertilizer designed for acid-loving plants.

You buy some flowers for your table: you tend them tenderly as you're able: You fetch them water from hither and thither – What thanks do you get for it all, They wither.

– Samuel Hoffenstein

CHANGE THE COLOR OF HYDRANGEA FLOWERS

The flowers of Bigleaf, H. macrophylla, can be either pink or blue. To make the flowers blue, dissolve a tablespoon of aluminum sulfate in a gallon of water and drench the soil around the plant in March, April and May. To make pink flowers, dissolve one tablespoon of hydrated lime in a gallon of water and drench the soil around the plant in March, April and May. Spilling the solution on the leaves may damage them.

HYDRANGEAS ARE EASY TO PROPAGATE

Rooting hydrangeas is easy on either old or new wood. Just bend a branch down to the soil, lightly scrape where it touches the soil, cover that with soil and mulch, then top with a brick. Leave about six to twelve inches of the tip growth uncovered. Keep it well watered. In a few weeks it will start roots under the brick. Then cut it from the mother tree, and you have another plant.

Oakleaf hydrangeas can be propagated easily from its seed. Collect the small dried seeds from the center of the cluster beneath large, outer florets, from November through January. Hundreds of tiny, brown seeds about the size of a half a grain of sand will fall out. Sprinkle the seeds in fine seed-starting potting soil. Do not cover them. Moisten the soil with a very fine mist of water. Place in a sunny spot where the air temperature is about 70 degrees. Seeds will sprout in about 18 days. When they are about one inch tall, transplant them to four inch pots. After five weeks, fertilize them with six pellets of 14-14-14 Osmocote, placed on top of the soil in each pot. When the seedlings are about four inches tall, pinch out the top to encourage branching. When roots fill the pot, you can plant the hydrangea outside.

Camellias

A camellia is one of the most rewarding plants you can grow. (I should make the word camellia plural, because once you start looking at the variety available, it will be impossible to have only one). It is not just that they bloom at a time when almost nothing is blooming, it is that they bloom in profusion and come in such a fabulous variety of shapes and sizes with a color range from white to pink to red, in solids or variegated varieties. The neat, glossy evergreen foliage is always attractive. A camellia can be used as a single specimen plant or grouped as a shrub border, in the background of perennial borders, or as an informal hedge. Most camellias will eventually grow into a large shrub or, if limbed up, into a small tree, but they can be kept pruned to a medium-size bush.

The plants are divided into early, middle and late bloomers, covering the period from November into April. They are superb as cut flowers. Individual blooms are beautiful floating in water, or you can fill a vase with branches covered in blooms.

The prime time to plant camellias is in the fall so that the roots can begin to get established during the winter, but it is possible to plant container-grown camellias when they are in bloom so you can see exactly what you are buying. Another wonderful idea is to buy camellias (look for good bud count) in November and place them in any empty urns or containers on your porch for the winter – they look great, bloom well and then when it is time to refill your containers with plants in the spring, take the camellias out and plant them in the landscape.

CAMELLIA FLOWER STYLE CLASSIFICATIONS

SINGLE FLOWER　　　DOUBLE　　　FORMAL　　　PEONY

Camellias prefer semi-shade with the optimum site the northern side of a building. The red-blooming varieties tolerate the most sun. (Note: those placed in sunny locations should be planted as young plants in very early spring so that they can grow to tolerate the sun). Camellias should be planted shallowly (no deeper than they are growing in the pot) in acid soil (which is plentiful in the Midlands) enriched with a heavy dose of compost. If you do not have good drainage you will also need to add sand along with the compost. They should be spaced 5 to 8 feet apart from trunk to trunk, depending on the growth habit of the particular plants you have. Once planted they should be mulched well to protect the roots, but leave four inches around the trunk uncovered so the trunk will stay dry. Water well the first few years (at least one inch a week) and then in future years, during dry spells. Camellias can also be grown in large planters in a protected place or with protection for the roots (blankets around the pot) when the temperature falls below 20 degrees.

Garden camellias are relatively disease-free. The worst problem can be petal blight (which causes brown blotches on the flowers), but this can be avoided by cleaning up all the dead petals and flowers from around the camellia. This is important since there is no cure for petal blight. One other bothersome problem can be white scale on the leaves. This can be prevented by painting a strip of Cygon around the base of the camellia in early spring (prepare yourself for the worst smell you can imagine!) or by spraying with dormant oil when the temperature is right. Camellias are pruned immediately after flowering. If you wait too long, you will be cutting off next year's blooms. Fertilize in the spring after flowering and again in June or use time release fertilizer only once right after flowering.

Old gardeners never die they just spade away.

– Muriel Cox

Most camellias that grow well in our area are of the camellia japonica variety or one of the Williamsii hybrids. If you really become a camellia enthusiast, you will find there are also varieties available that can be used in hanging baskets, espaliered, grown as standards, in window boxes and as ground-covers. The difficulty lies in figuring out which will do well in our climate. Many camellias are for growing in greenhouses, therefore not in the landscape because the flower buds would be damaged by the cold – but there are many, many others which will do well.

Some of the local favorites are Alba Plena, Aspasia MacArthur, all the Betty Sheffield varieties, Debutante (originally propagated at Magnolia Gardens in Charleston), Dr. Tinsley, Doncklarii, all the Elegans varieties, Glen Forty, Governor Mouton, Herme, Lady Clare, Mathotiana, Mathotiana Supreme, Nuccio's Gem, Professor Sargent, R. L. Wheeler, Seafoam, Valentines's Day and Valentine's Day variegated (this is actually one of the few varieties of Camellia Reticulata that can be grown in this area), Victory White, Ville de Nantes, and White Empress.

Of course, part of the adventure may be finding your own list of selections to try. Local nurseryman can be called on for advice as well as can the multitude of books on camellias in the public library. Don't miss <u>Growing Camellias</u> by Margaret Tapley and <u>The Illustrated Encyclopedia of Camellias</u> by Stirling Macoboy. The Camellia Forest Nursery in Chapel Hill, North Carolina (www.Camforest.com) does considerable work in finding cold-hardy camellias for the landscape. Coopers Nursery in Columbia will take requests for specific plants and see if their suppliers carry them. They will need your list by the end of July. The very best way to get information is to join a local camellia society. For information, contact the American Camellia Society at www.Camellias-acs.com. For dues of about $10 a year, you can go to meetings on pruning, grafting, propagation, "gibing" for huge early blooms (some societies supply each member with the gibberellic acid), and cut flower use, and meet a very interesting group of dedicated camellia growers who are extremely willing to share the knowledge from their many years of experience.

Note: *Don't forget the Camellia Sasanqua. These are the fall blooming camellias and make wonderful specimen plants or hedges. They tolerate full sun or shade. Sasanqua have a very heavy bloom and come in a variety of colors and forms, but the cut flowers do not last.*

WAXING CAMELLIAS

Preserving camellia blooms by dipping them in wax is a process that lets their form and beautiful color be enjoyed for one to three weeks. They will then turn golden brown and will last for years. Once dry, they can be sprayed gold or silver and used for holiday decorations.

Items Needed

Large double boiler **(never heat wax without one)**
Candy thermometer with clip
Two pounds of wax (canning section of grocery)
Large container of ice water (dish pan or sink)
Very fresh camellia blooms-no ants or bruises

- Cut stems one inch long with one or two leaves if desired.
- Clip thermometer to the top of the double boiler.
- Add wax and melt over boiling water. The wax will register 170 -180 degrees when melted.
- Remove from heat and cool to 136-138 degrees. Keep covered to prevent skin forming.
- Start with darkest blooms.
- Grasp bloom by the stem and dip in wax with a slight twisting motion.
- Place **immediately** in ice water for 5 minute⁻
- When cool, place on paper towels to drain.

Handle blooms carefully. Store in a cool place. They make lovely table decorations, look great floating in punch and make good gifts for sick friends because they require no water.

And beauty is not a need but an ecstacy...
A garden for ever in bloom and a flock of angels for ever in flight.

— Kahlil Gibran

Roses,
THE WORLD'S MOST POPULAR FLOWER

Man's love for and attraction to roses is older than recorded time. Lush walled gardens were created thousands of years ago in Persia, wrestled from the deserts and winds, and protected from enemies and wild animals. Roses and water were important parts of these first gardens. Fast-flowing canals were edged with roses highly prized for their colors and fragrance. Roses traveled the earth by way of early traders following caravan routes. Persia's Damasks were taken to India and China and to the west into the Mediterranean. In Morocco great perfume industries have flourished for centuries using the Damask rose. The perfumeries of France have used the Centifolia Rose for centuries. It is an essential element of Chanel #5, Shalamar, Joy, White Linen and many other perfumes.

THE SOUL OF A ROSE

History shows that among flowers, the rose has always reigned supreme. It is the emblem of our deepest feelings of love. One can't speak of roses without showing some degree of passion. Roses have always inspired man's creative and sensual side. The varieties to be found in the rose world are endless.

Species of roses usually have just five petals. They often bloom only once a season but sometimes more. They are enchanting on a trellis or over a doorway where they ramble and sprawl with abandon. These original roses require little maintenance and need to be used more in our gardens.

Who loves not roses, knows not beauty's smile;
Romance hath spurned him - Poetry passed him by.

There are as many as 170 species of roses native to North America. It is appropriate that the rose is our national flower. Old Garden roses are those groups of roses cultivated before 1867. They include the Gallicas, Damasks, Albas, Centifolias, Mosses, Bourbons, Chinas, Noisettes and others. There are new varieties of these old roses developed after 1867. Because they are disease resistant, hardy, and strongly fragrant old roses are experiencing a resurgence of popularity. Highly recommended for our Southern gardens, these old roses bring character and history to our home gardens. The Noisette was developed in Charleston, SC. We need to grow it more!

Modern roses are those introduced after 1867. They are the most popular and widely grown roses today and are quite diverse including the hybrid teas, hybrid perpetuals, Rugosa, Climbers, Ramblers, Polyanthus, Florabundas, Grandifloras, Miniatures and English Roses. The choices are mind boggling. These are the roses that require the most care but their high petal count, beautiful flower form and spectacular colors lure the gardener time and again.

As well as rose beds, consider using roses in perennial borders. Avoid the demanding ones like the hybrid teas and choose shrub or ground cover types. The varieties are endless. Heat tolerant roses for the South that are disease resistant can be a bonanza in any of our yards. Go for it!

Roses do not compete successfully with roots from neighboring plants so place them carefully. Sunshine is a must - minimum of 6-8 hours daily with some afternoon shade to prevent fading of the flowers in the hot humid long growing season of Columbia. Most of the modern roses need weekly spraying with fungicides, insecticides and miticedes. The cost of these chemicals can be high. Choices more acceptable to the environment are also available. Whatever is used please add a product like Indicate 5 to the spray water. It adjusts the Ph of the water and facilitates the penetrating, wetting, and spreading of the solutions used. Also add liquid fertilizer to the spray water, such as miracle gro for roses 15-30-15 or Carl Pool rose fertilizer. These two additions to the spray formula (fertilizer and Ph adjuster) will make a huge difference in the success of the roses and the leaves.

The world is a rose: smell it and pass it on to your friends.

— Persian Proverb

Roses

Remember that roses are heavy feeders and drinkers – they need organic materials dug into their soil in the spring. Granular fertilizer at regular intervals is needed all summer long and liquid food either in the spray or applied alone. Chelated iron once a month during the growing season and Epsom Salt 3-4 tablespoons per bush is also needed. Stop fertilizing in the middle of September. The drinking part – they of course need lots of water and good drainage. Remember to supplement the rain. A drip system is preferable to sprinkle irrigation because wetting the bushes promotes the fungal growth that we so abhor.

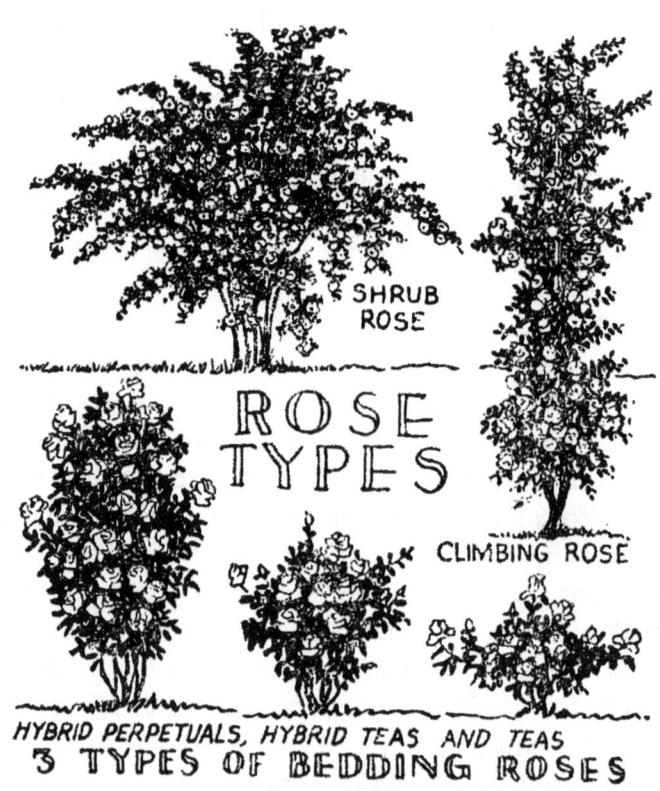

> We can complain because rose bushes have thorns,
> or rejoice because thorn bushes have roses.
>
> – Abraham Lincoln

Becoming a member of the Greater Columbia Rose Society, the South Carolina Rose Society and the American Rose Society will further one's passion for roses, add knowledge and camaraderie.

It is advisable for anyone who applies pesticides to become a certified spray applicator. Workshops are available through the Clemson Extension service.

DRYING ROSES

Pick a rose bud or one that is just barely open. Bake in oven at a very low heat — about 200 degrees, and keep the door propped open. Leave in oven about five hours. Remove leaves and thorns after it is completely cooled. You may also dead head, and spread loosely in baskets and air dry naturally inside.

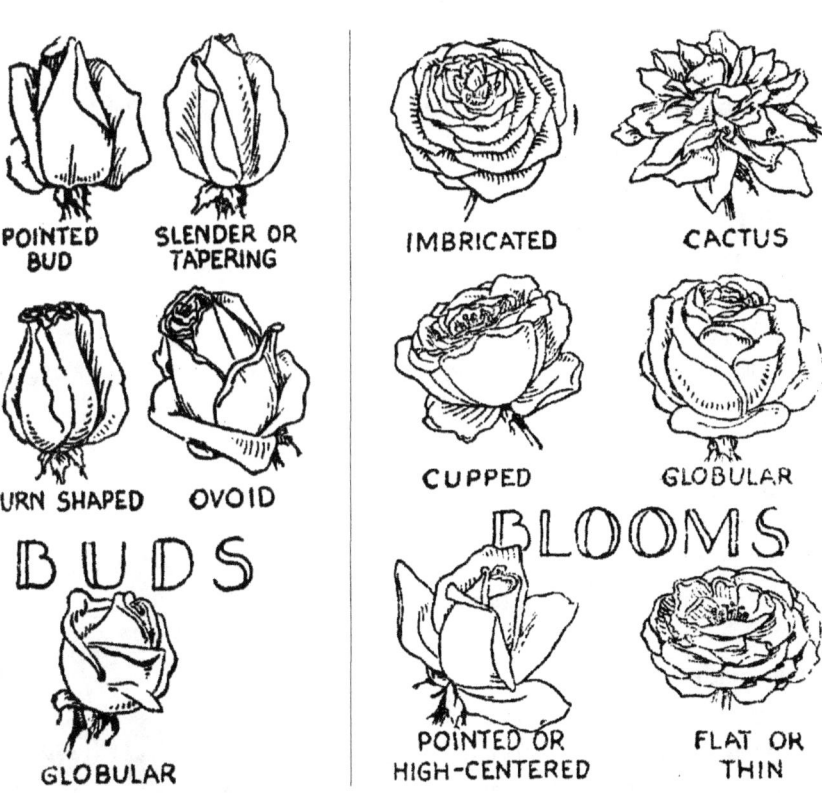

Rosaries were made of pulverized rose petals.

MONTHLY CARE OF ROSES:

Pat Henry; Roses Unlimited, Laurens S. C.
rosesunlmt@aol.com
www.roseunlimitedownroot.com

November/December:
Use manure or mushroom compost around all bushes. Put 1 cup super phosphate on each plant; put the phosphate 8 to 10 inches around the plant from the base. Leave the leaves on the roses all winter.

End of February:
Prune roses. After pruning, use 1 cup dolominic lime and 1/2 cup Epsom salt on each rose bush. Work into the soil.

Mid-March:
On established roses, use 1 cup 10-10-10 granular fertilizer (Rainbow is a good brand) and work this into the soil.

April 1:
Mills Magic Mix - 2 cups around each bush worked into soil.

Mid April:
Begin liquid feeding with Easy Feed. Use 1 gallon per each rose bush. Feed every 30 days through September.

Fungicide:
Bannermax and Manzate 200 (it is a powder, mix with hot water and then add to Bannermax) and Indicate 5 for good pH, spray every 3 weeks. Spray under the leaves and on top of the plant.

Insecticide:
NEVER MIX FUNGICIDE AND INSECTICIDE!!
Orthene Powder, use 2 teaspoons to a gallon of water.
Spray over the tops (buds) of the plants.
Good for getting rid of thrips.

Web sites:
rosemania.com

Another Rose Gardeners Fertilizer Program

- Always water plants before applying fertilizer. Water roots and not leaves.

- After the first pruning: granular 16-4-8 fertilizer.

- After subsequent prunings: an organic mixture such as Eco-Joy or Mills Magic. 2-3 cups per bush.

- When buds are pea size: apply the above organic mixture.

Also during the growing season:

- First week: Miracle-Gro for roses, 1 Tablespoon per gallon of water.

- Second week: Fish emulsion, 1 Tablespoon/gallon water.

- Third week: Epson salts, one fourth cup per bush.

- Fourth week: Alfafa tea, which should be made in a big container (30 gal.) like a trash can. Add 8-10 cups of Alfafa meal or pellets. Fill with water, stir once a day for three days. Let set for two days. Use. Fill and repeat process second time.

- One week before a show or party, use Shultz Bloom Plus (10-60-10), instead of Miracle-Gro. This speeds up blooming, and enhances the blooms size and color

The Yard! The Grass! The Lawn! The Turf!

Nature never intended for one and only one plant to thrive all year long through drenching rains, drought, humidity, extreme heat and winter freezes with no invasion of disease or insects in a place we call the GRASS. Therefore, in choosing grass we must carefully consider the needs of the various types as well as our level of commitment toward achieving the desired result. The warm-season grasses — centipede, hybrid bermuda and zoysia — are best suited to the conditions in the South Carolina Midlands.

- **CENTIPEDE**
  Choice of most Midlands' homeowners, slow-growing, heat tolerant, low maintenance, more shade tolerant than Bermuda, but less shade-tolerant than zoysia, tolerates low fertilization and drought fairly well. Susceptible to winter kill during extremely cold weather. Does not tolerate compaction, excessive thatch, or heavy shade.

- **HYBRID BERMUDA**
  Most predominate species throughout the South. Salt tolerant, heat tolerant, tolerant to drought and traffic and intolerant of shade. Highest degree of maintenance, i.e. frequent close mowing, regular fertilization, edging and de-thatching.

- **ZOYSIA**
  Adapts well from Midlands to coast. One of most cold-tolerant of warm-season grasses. Forms very dense lawn, requiring less mowing than others. Tolerates cold temperatures, shade and salt spray and heat. Susceptible to drought. Does best in upper South.

- **ST. AUGUSTINE (CHARLESTON GRASS)**
  Best suited to the hot humid conditions of the SC Low Country. It is becoming more popular because of its tolerance to shade, but it will not thrive under trees.

The ideal time for planting warm-season grasses is during late spring (April-May). The roots are actively growing then (dormancy has been broken) and the long growing season is ahead, thus creating the best chance for successful coverage. Sodding creates an instant lawn but is often more expensive. Plugs (sprigs) and seeds can also produce good results in time. New plantings should never be allowed to dry out while they are establishing.

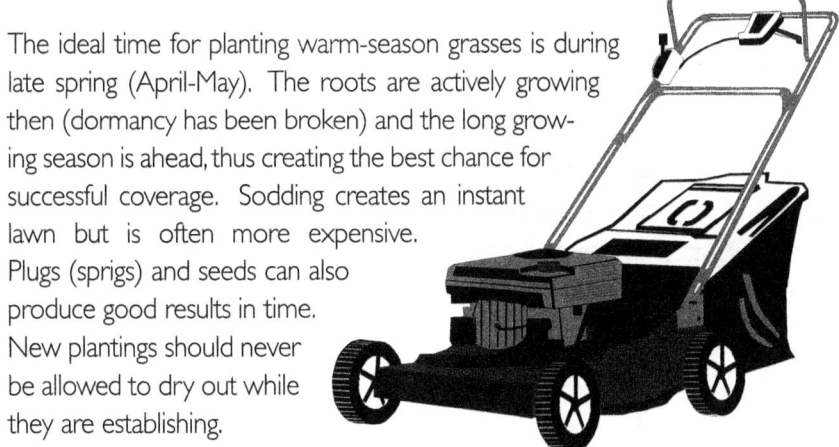

A soil test should be done periodically to determine the needs of an established lawn (and certainly before a new one is planted). The Clemson Extension Service can do this for you. The results will provide the type of fertilizer most suitable, as well as exact amounts and times of applications for your lawn.

Generally speaking, centipede will grow well with 2 applications of fertilizer; one during the first two weeks in May (not before!) and another application in mid-summer. Three to four pounds per 1000 square feet of 15-0-15 or 16-4-8 or any other fertilizer with a similar ratio will suffice. Mow centipede as needed to 1.5 inches and return clippings to lawn.

Over watering centipede is its biggest problem. Irrigation systems set on a predetermined schedule regardless of rainfall are often the culprit. During droughts, water 1 inch of water per week in the early morning. To determine this rate, set a small container under the sprinkler and measure or mount a rain gauge in the planting area. Core aeration during the first part of June is a real plus for an established lawn. It improves drainage, relieves compaction, and stimulates new root growth.

E-mail reminder service for lawn fertilizing: www.scotts.com
All you do is enter your zipcode and grass type and they will remind you what to do, by email, at the appropriate time.

He that works without tools is twice tired.
– Benjamin Franklin

Herbs

Herbs are a garden world of excitement and intense sensory delight. They are among Mother Nature's oldest garden gifts. These easy-to-grow plants have been cultivated for centuries by gardeners who have found them to be medical necessities, culinary enhancements, unique landscape subjects and fragrant houseplants. Overall, herbs are very easy to grow. They can be arranged in flowerbeds, borders, containers, rock gardens, or assembled in a "formal kitchen garden."

- **LOCATION:**
  Herbs need sun. Six hours of good sunlight is standard, but some sun loving herbs do well in shady places; they just do not flower. Some of the thinner leaf herbs appreciate some afternoon shade.

- **SOIL AND FERTILIZER:**
  Herbs have shallow roots and need to be in a soil that has good drainage. Use raised beds if you have drainage problems. Usually one inch of water per week is sufficient, but let the ground dry out between waterings. Most soils in S.C. will produce excellent crops, but medium fertile soil is best for maximum aroma. Heavy applications of manure or high nitrogen content fertilizer will result in luxuriant foliage, but with no flavor. Before planting, dig soil to a 12-inch depth, adding lots of sand, aged manure, peat moss and compost as rotted leaves or grass clippings. Neutral soil with a pH of 6-7.5 is best.

- **PLANTING:**
  Plant herbs after the last spring frost date. Basil does not like temperatures below 45 degrees. Space herbs so each plant gets good air circulation and light to prevent disease and promote good growth. Herbs do well in pots but those need more attention than those in the ground.

- **HARVESTING:**
  For great oils, keep the flowers pinched off. Harvest herbs in the morning just after the dew has dried but before the sun gets hot. The concentration of essential oils is the highest at this time. Never cut the stem to the

ground; leave at least one-third of the stem/plant to grow back. The more it is cut, the more the plant will bush out. Stop large harvests on perennial herbs in late summer so the new growth can harden before winter.

TIPS:

- Fresh-cut herbs, wrapped in a damp towel and kept in a plastic bag, will keep several days in the refrigerator. For longer storage, fresh herbs can be packed in oil, vinegar, salt, mixed with butter, frozen or dried. Store oils and butter in the refrigerator.

- The simplest way to dry herbs is to tie several cut stems together in a bunch. Then hang the bunch, covered with a brown paper bag, punched with several holes, until dry, usually 10-14 days. The bag prevents the herbs from picking up dust and losing too much color. Store dried herbs in glass jars.

- Fresh herbs may be used in place of dried. Substitute 1 TABLESPOON fresh herbs for every TEASPOON of dried and cut salt in half.

Don't judge each day by the harvest you reap, but by the seeds you plant.

— R. L. Stevenson

HERB LIST

BASIL - Annual. Likes full sun and well-draining soil. Sensitive to cold. Height: 2 feet. Pick leaves off throughout the season to encourage bushiness. Pick flower heads off at the end of the season for a longer harvest. Good on everything, especially salads and tomatoes.

ROSEMARY - Perennial. Likes full sun to partial shade and well-draining soil. Likes soil to be on the dry side. Height: 5-6 feet. Can be left outside all winter in the South. Slow grower. Strong piney scent. Flowers and leaves edible. Good on beef, chicken, eggs, lamb, pork, fruit, peas, potatoes, and tomatoes.

THYME - Perennial. Likes full sun to partial shade and well-draining soil. Plant in location that gets afternoon shade. Height: 1 foot. Once established, is a good spreader but not invasive. Good on everything.

PARSLEY - Biannual. Likes moderately rich, moist, well-draining soil. Plant in full sun to partial shade. Plant in area where it will get afternoon shade. Height: 18 inches tall. Good on beef, chicken, eggs, lamb, fish, veal, potatoes, soups and tomatoes.

SAGE - Perennial. Plant in moderately rich, well-draining soil and in full sun. Height: 12-30 inches. Good on beef, chicken, eggs, fish, lamb, pork, and vegetables.

CHIVES - Perennial. Likes moderately rich, well-drained soil and in full sun. Height: 18 inches. Blooms in June and blossoms can be eaten. Do not chop before freezing. Good with chicken, eggs, fish and most vegetables.

DILL - Hardy annual. Likes moderately rich, well-drained soil and full sun. Grows to about 3 feet tall. Attracts Swallow Tail Butterfly caterpillars. Leaves and seeds are used. Will seed in mid to late summer. Excellent on fish, eggs, chicken and most vegetables.

OREGANO - Perennial. Plant in average, well-draining soil and full sun. Grows 1-2 feet tall. Great in Italian dishes, pizza, tomatoes and most meats.

MINT - Perennial. Likes rich, moist, well-draining soils. Plant in full sun to partial shade. Very invasive plant that will spread if allowed. To contain its spreading, plant in a large plastic pot then place pot in the ground with top 2 inches showing or plant in containers. Good for teas, jellies, fruit, green beans, carrots and lamb.

MEXICAN TARRAGON - Much hardier than French tarragon. Mexican Tarragon is an annual and will grow about 3 feet. It likes full sun and well-draining soil. It has lovely flowers in mid summer. Leaves are used for cooking. Good for vinegars, meats, asparagus, broccoli, carrots, peas, potatoes, rice and tomatoes. To make tarragon vinegar, steep tarragon sprigs in white wine vinegar.

LAVENDER - Perennial. There are several types of lavender but the French lavender (Lavandula dentata) grows best here. It likes average, well-draining soil. It prefers a slightly higher pH around 7.0-7.2 so give the plants a little lime every two years or so. It grows best with morning sun and afternoon shade. Use for potpourris, cookies, fruits and sorbets.

Windowsill Herbs

What could be more convenient than delicious herbs in your window during the cold winter months? The more light your herbs get, the happier they'll be. A south-facing window is the best, and they enjoy the humidity of a laundry room, bathroom or above a sink. Do not let the leaves touch the window glass. Do not fertilize much. But the main requirement is correct watering. Over watering is the most common killer. Many gardeners water when the top soil is dry to the touch, but remember, the roots may still be wet, so water when the soil pulls away from the pot. Do not let your herbs completely dry out or stand in water. When harvesting, clip what you need, but always leave green growth on the plant.

Good Herbs for indoors: chives, cilantro (Vietnamese or Mexican), thyme, bay, sage, winter savory, winter tarragon, oregano, parsley, savory and mint.

He has no yard behind his house,
No garden green to till,
And so he works the hothouse plan
Upon his windowsill.

— Old Song

Edible Flowers

Edible flowers are not a new fad. The Romans used roses and violets to flavor wine, and the Aztecs mixed marigolds with chocolate. But be careful that any flower you eat, or that even touches, what you are going to eat, has not been exposed to pesticides, herbicides, or fungicides.

POPULAR BITES FROM THE FLOWER GARDEN:

- **Violets, Pansies** - slightly sweet, sometimes peppery flavor. Beautiful decoration on cakes.

- **Nasturtiums** - crispy, spicy flavor. Wonderful in martinis. Good in salad dressings.

- **Marigolds** - adds saffron-like color. Mix with butter and spread on muffins.

- **Roses** - fruity flavor. Create rosewater. Sprinkle on desserts and salads.

- **Squash Blossoms** - mild squash flavor, great in pastas. Stuff with mozzarella, then batter and fry.

- **Lavender** - mild floral and herbal flavor. Freeze blossoms in ice cubes to add to summer drinks.

Other flowers to try: chrysanthemum, daylily, geranium, gardenia, daisy.

Flower-based teas are a summertime treat. Use 2 or 3 teaspoons of fresh or dried petals per cup of boiling water. Steep the petals in the water for 3 to 8 minutes, as you prefer. Strain and serve hot.

A delicious spread is made by adding chopped petals or leaves to mild honey. A good combination is 1/3 cup flowers to 1 cup honey. Put mixture in a jar, then set it in 3 inches of boiling water, gently boil for about half an hour. Cool and store for 2 weeks before serving. It is ambrosia, served on toast.

DO NOT EAT THESE TOXIC FLOWERS.

Be careful of these common poisonous plants that may be in your garden:

Daffodil, Hydrangea, Tulip, Morning Glory, Iris, Poinsettia, Yellow Jessamin, Holly, Mistletoe, Pokeberry, Boxwood, Ivy, Oleander, Azalea, Easter Lily, Wisteria, and the leaf, stem or bark of the tomato. To be safe, teach children not to eat anything in the garden (or houseplants – especially peace lilies, philodendrom). Remove mushrooms from your yard and be careful of the sticks used to skewer marshmallows. Keep the Poison Control Centers' number in a handy place.

In South Carolina the number is (800) 922-1117
The national number is (800) 222-1222.

Thyme began in the garden.

Bulbs

"Tell all" about bulbs in a page or two? Impossible! What we will do, however, is provide you with fundamentals about bulbs in general, and then direct you to resources for more in-depth information.

What we typically refer to as bulbs may actually be corms, tubers or rhizomes – all of which sound like diseases of the foot but are, in fact, underground plant parts which store energy and produce blooms. Bulbs are likely our most enduring plants, coming back year after year and producing a myriad of blooms in all colors, sizes and varieties.

Bulbs may be planted in beds or containers, and require a minimum of care. If you are a "neat freak," however, consider carefully before you plant them anywhere because the number one rule of bulbs is: do not bend, fold, staple, twist, braid, or cut the foliage until it has turned yellow and wilted. Now this may take awhile, 6-12 weeks, during which time the leaves/blades are lying atop perennials struggling to push through, or covering prime spots for annual plantings. Your garden may appear as if the Jolly Green Giant has been doing the Monster Mash throughout, but the foliage must be left alone to absorb energy and transmit it to the bulbs so you will have magnificent blooms the following year. If you are determined in spite of the mess, read on!

The only thing I grow in my garden is tired.

GENERAL RULES OF THUMB FOR BULBS:

- **Soil:** It should be loose and porous, well-drained, and moisture retentive. You might mix coarse sand or fine gravel with the soil.

- **Spacing:** Plant in irregular masses instead of in straight lines or scattered singly throughout your bed. Refer to planting instructions for specific bulbs for proper spacing within the masses.

- **Depth:** The hole should be about three times as deep as the bulb's greatest diameter. If planting lots of bulbs, you may find it more efficient to dig trenches or excavate a whole area than to dig one hole at a time.

- **Fertilizer:** At planting time, work a complete bulb fertilizer into the soil. You may use a side-dressing of a bulb booster at the start of blooming season. In all cases, it is most important to fertilize after bloom time with a bulb fertilizer that is high in nitrogen, phosphorous and potassium.

- **Watering:** Soak thoroughly at planting time. Water deeply throughout the blooming season.

- **Mulch:** As you should do with all plants

- **Cutting:** When cutting flower stalks either to enjoy indoors or as they fade, remember to leave as much foliage as possible.

Space and light and order, these ae the things men need, as much as they need bread.

— Le Corbusier

Bulbs

As Jim Wilson says in his S.C. Gardener's Guide, "tulips, the most popular flowers grown from bulbs, are not often seen in South Carolina because they require colder, longer winters than we have at most elevations." A former Columbia Garden Club horticulture chairman says, "Tulips prefer to be planted in December, that is, re-planted every December!" The message is that tulips do not return successfully in our South Carolina area, so look instead to the many other bulbs that do thrive here. Treat tulips as annuals here.

Daffodils are good choices for the Midlands. Robbie Bella Fontaine refers to the daffodil lists in *The Southern Gardner's Book of Lists* for the best daffodils for the South.

THESE ARE SOME OF THEIR FAVORITE DAFFODILS

LARGE:	MINIATURES:
Carlton	Baby Moon
Ceylon	Hawera
February Gold	Peeping Tom
Fortune	Professor Einstein
Gigantic Star	Tete-a-Tete
Ice Follies	

As for bulbs other than daffodils, we recommend blue-purple and white large-flowering crocus, the grape hyacinth Muscari (but they are short-lived in our garden), Scilla siberica, Dutch iris (beautiful cut flowers, but foliage hangs around until late spring), Calla lilies, and August Rain Lilies.

She gadereth floures, party white and rede,
To make a subtil gerland for hire hede
And as an aungel hevenysshly she soong.

— Chaucer

We also recommend Lycoris radiata. They bloom in the fall with few competitors. Plant them with Asiatic jasmine. Other suggestions are elephant ears (they multiply and like wet spots), snowdrops, snow flakes, and of course, the intensely fragrant ginger lilies (these are messy and should be planted out of the way, maybe by the trash can!)

MISCELLANEOUS BULB TIPS

- To keep chipmunks and other critters from eating your bulbs, invert a plastic berry basket over bulbs at planting time and then cover with soil. Or, contain your bulbs in chicken wire before planting.

- Daffodil sap can harm other flowers, put them in water alone, before combining with other flowers.

- Irises should not be planted in the shade or near other plants.

SOURCES FOR BULBS
- Brent & Becky's Bulbs, Gloucester, VA (804)693-3966
- Van Engelen, Bantam CT (860)567-8734
- Van Bourgondien, Babylon, NY (800)622-9997
- Dutch Gardens, Adelphia, NJ (800)818-3861

INTERNET SITES
- www.dutchbulbs.com
- www.gardennet.com
- www.myseasons.com
- www.bulblady.com
- www.bulb.com

A weed is no more than a flower in disguise.

— James Russell Lowell

Heirloom Plants

Who can forget the hypnotic fragrance of an old-fashioned rose tucked away in the corner of grandmother's garden of yesteryear? Today, the memory of that rose in her garden may bring a longing for the gardens and plants of the past. There is a certain nostalgia for heritage plants or pass-along plants. Heritage plants definitely last! You can find examples, such as heritage roses and daffodils, at old homes sites throughout our region. If these specimens still exist in a garden without any care after a hundred years, you know they are tough, drought-resistent, and disease-resistant! Often, old varieties of plants possess other, more ephemeral, characteristics like the sweet scent of the fragrant tea olive or the bright beauty of a magenta gladiolus.

If you want to cultivate old treasures, heritage seeds and plants can be found at such local sources as Wayside Gardens in Hodges and Woodlanders Nursery in Aiken. Historic Monticello in Virginia also offers historic flower and vegetable seeds. Or, if you have a plant from your grandmother's garden, share it with another but don't expect a thank you note. Following an old Southern saying, the plant will not grow if an expression of appreciation is given.

Explore heritage landscapes. We are blessed with many historic and/or restored landscapes in South Carolina: Middleton Place, Magnolia Gardens, and Brookgreen Gardens, to name a few. In Columbia, our own Woodrow Wilson Boyhood Home represents a garden of the Victorian period and displays many plants from that era. When traveling, visit Colonial Williamsburg's nursery and Monticello's gardens.

Historic landscapes and plants are a vital part of our Southern cultural heritage. Preserve a special old bulb or shrub, and you will be greatly rewarded for your horticultural efforts!

Christy Snipes Bowers, M.L.A., is a historic landscape consultant in the Midlands S.C. area.

> *Nature soon takes over if the gardener is absent.*
> — Penelope Hobhouse

ORNAMENTAL HERITAGE PLANTS

- **Trees:**
  Crape myrtle - Lagerstroemia indica
  Deodar Cedar - Cedrus deodar
  Magnolia-grandiflora - Southern magnolia
  Live-Oak - Quercus virginiana

- **Shrubs:**
  Boxwood - Buxus sempervirens
  Flowering quince - Chaenomeles speciosa
  Oakleaf hydrangea - Hydrangea quercifolia
  Mock-orange - Philadelphus coronarius
  Scotch broom - Cytisus scoparius

- **Heritage Vines:**
  Coral honeysuckle - Lonicera sempervirens
  Five-leaf Akebia - Akebia Quinta
  Confederate jasmine - Trachelospermum jasminoides
  Sweet autumn clematis - Clematis paniculata

- **Ground Covers:**
  Bigleaf periwinkle - Vinca major
  Little-leaf periwinkle - Vinca minor

- **Bulbs:**
  Naked ladies - Lycoris species
  Old-fashioned daffodil - Narcissus species
  Snowflakes or snowdrops - Leucojum species

- **Annual & Perennials:**
  Cosmos - Cosmos bipinnatus (A)
  Ginger lily - Hedychium coronarium (P)
  Old-fashioned daylily - Hemerocallis species (P)
  Spiderwort - Tradescantia virginiana (P)
  Wild Ageratum - Eupatorium coelestinum (P)

All gardens are a form of autobiography.
— Robert Dash

Container Gardening

Big impact, less plants (and therefore less investment of time and money), very little maintenance, transportable...yes, it is the perfect garden. It is container gardening, and it can solve a lot of gardening problems. Here are some hints to have fabulous containers of flowers all year long

The bigger the container, the better. Use a deep container with a wide mouth, at least 24 inches in diameter.

Don't forget window boxes.

Use your imagination to think of something fun in which to plant your container garden. Perhaps you have an old, broken toy wagon or a bucket with holes which you were going to discard. Or, go to garage sales and antique malls and look for interesting shapes and finishes.

Indoor plant departments have interesting tropicals.

Perennials can be replanted in the garden when you change out the container.

Chose plants that all like the same conditions. *(Sun or shade, wet or dry)*

Clean used containers each year to eliminate bacteria and replace soil.

Frequent watering is one problem with containers. They do dry out faster than your in-ground garden so you must make sure they are properly watered. Drainage holes are a must. If the containers are out of the rain or if the rain is not adequate then arrange containers near a water source. They can also be attached to an existing sprinkler system.

A garden is never so good as it will be next year.

—Thomas Cooper

Feeding is essential to keep containers in peak bloom. Constant watering diminishes the supply of fertilizer so fertilize once a week with a liquid fertilizer such as 15-30-15 (Bloom buster) the first month. BUT, they can be over fertilized. If not sure, it is better to underfeed. Clues for over fertilization are chalky deposits on pots, plants with weak stems, an excess of leaves and a general flimsiness to them. Never fertilize plants when soil is dry and leaves are wilted.

Root pruning solves the problem of container plants that have gotten out of control. Cut back no more than one-third of the tips of the roots, and then plant in the same size pot but with more soil. Do not root prune when the plant is growing, usually mid-summer.

RECIPE FOR PLANTING SOIL:
3 parts soil-less planting mix, (such as Peter's, Metro Mix, Majestic), and 1 part mushroom compost or composted manure. Add a couple handfuls of slow release granular fertilizer such as Osmocote. It is also a good idea to add water retention granules to the potting mix.

TO PLANT:
- Bottom Layer: Place gravel, shards of clay pots or plastic packing peanuts for a slightly lighter-weight container should you need to move it.
- Fill with soil mix, but leave room at the top of the pot for watering.
- Mulch top with soil conditioner to retain moisture during the summer.

All my hurts, my garden spade can heal.
— Ralph Waldo Emerson

PLANT CHOICES FOR CONTAINERS:
- A good place to use invasive plants you can not let loose in your garden like mints, ivy and bamboo.
- Annuals are a good choice because they bloom.
- Consider trying grasses, tropicals, vines and shrubs such as sasanquas, tea olive, variegated euonymus.
- Bulbs: over-plant with other bloomers
- Trees: Christmas tree shaped evergreens – add lights for the holidays or any night!
- Herbs: parsley, rosemary
- Vegetables: kale, lettuce, Swiss chard, red mustard
- Containers dry out quickly (especially terra cotta) so drought tolerant plants make a good choice.

COMPOSITION:
- Try for three heights of plants:
  Tall: Plant in center or at the back, ornamental grass such miscanthus; canna, Chinese fan palm, African iris, sword fern, or salvia
  Medium fillers: penta, lantana, plumbago, caladiums, coleus, impatiens, hosta or begonias
  Cascading (trailing over edge): verbena, lantana, coreopsis, trailing zinnia, ivy, vinca major, petunia
- The total height of plants should be approximately the height of the container.
- Keep the following in mind: The more varied the plants, the more interesting the composition. Use a variety of tall, spiky, rounded, and trailing plants for visual interest.
- Variegated plants add depth.
- Fill the container. It is good to crowd.

(See also flower arranging in this book.)

Some Columbia container experts are Ruthie Lacey and Rebekah's Garden at the State Farmer's Market.

Patience is a flower that grows not in every garden.

SAMPLE FLOWERS FOR CONTAINERS:

Sun: African iris(tall), penta, lantana, gold baby English ivy, geranium, plumbago, variegated plectranthus, Gypsophila (filler), verbena "Tapier pink", petunia integrifolia (perennial), asparagus fern, lobelia, variegated ivy

Shade: Begonia, caladiums, hosta, impatiens, Japanese painted fern, ivy, small hydrangea, ferns, impatiens

Mixed sun: impatiens, petunias, strawberry begonia, ajuga, variegate euonymus.

An example of a pot which changes with the seasons:

Permanent – variegated aspidistra & green ivy;
For Summer – coleus, caladiums, Impatiens
For Fall – urly-leaved green and white kale, variegated glacier ivy, white pansies
For Winter – tall tulips (for spring bloom), over planted with pansies & Korean rock fern

*Plants in pots are like animals in a zoo –
they are totally dependent on their keepers*

— John Van De Water

EASY-TO-GROW, HARD-TO-KILL
Houseplants

- **CAST-IRON PLANT:**
  Tall upright leaves which are wonderful in cut flower arrangements. Try spiking the stem through the leaf for a fun loop in your arrangement. Can tolerate low light, dry air, almost anything except over-watering. It is also a good evergreen addition in your garden.

- **PEACE LILY:**
  Cluster of pointed long leaves. Tolerates a wide range of conditions but prefers steadily moist soil. It scorches in direct sun. May have white or pink blooms.

- **GOLDEN POTHOS:**
  Gold-streaked, heart-shaped bright green leaves. Water to prevent wilting, but allow soil to dry between waterings. Pinch back to branch the vines.

- **RUBBER TREE:**
  Large, leathery leaves which can get very tall. Prune. Needs bright indirect light and moist soil.

- **SPIDER PLANT:**
  Clump of lance-like flexible leaves that are perfect in hanging baskets. It does best in bright light with regular watering. The baby plants it bears on long stems quickly root in water or soil.

- **MOTHER-IN-LAW'S TONGUE:**
  Clump of stiff, erect, lance-shaped leaves. Be careful of the sharp points at the end of the leaves. If they are damaged, the leaf stops growing. Otherwise, very easy to grow.

Everything is good in its season.

— Italian Proverb

Coastal Gardening

The obstacles facing coastal gardens are salt spray, wind and sandy soil.

The following tips should help:

- Every gardener should test his/her soil. At the coast one should also test the water. Since so much of the water comes from wells, it may have too much salt for healthy plants.

- Protect plants from strong winds. A tree/shrub wind break may be needed. Keep in mind that wind is very drying to plants.

- Sandy soil will need amendments to retain moisture. Raised beds which can be easily amended are helpful.

- Generously mulch with material that will not blow away.

- Protect plants from the intense scorching sun.

- Use St. Augustine sod.

Some reliable coastal trees and plants:
elaeagnus, oleander, yaupon & American holly, wax myrtle, pittosporum, viburnum, yucca, pines, cherry laurel, live oaks (Oh, yes, S.C. needs many more), cabbage palm, lantana, daylilies, daffodils, many ornamental grasses like pampas, miscanthus, fountain, and most annuals if they are protected. And do think tropicals – even if they get the odd winter freeze it is usually so mild that they recover.

> *Prim little scholars are the flowers of her garden,*
> *Trained to stand in rows, and asking if they please.*
> *I might love them well but for loving more the wild ones –*
> *O my wild ones! They tell me more than these.*
> — George Meredith

Birds

Suet is a high energy food that birds love and need more in the spring and summer during the nesting season. You can now buy a year-round suet cake that does not melt or get rancid in the hot summer. The suet cage should be constructed of plastic-coated wire and hung from the branch of a tree 6 to 8 feet off the ground.

Not all birds use birdhouses. Many build their own nests. However, bluebirds, titmice, chickadees, wrens and purple martins are some of the birds that use birdhouses. Birdhouses should be cleaned each year before breeding season begins in the winter.

GOOD BOOKS ON BIRDS ARE:
- *Peterson Field Guide – Eastern Birds*
- *Birds of the Carolinas*

My garden, weed it and reap.

Birds

Birds are fascinating, beautiful, colorful acrobats, and a joy to watch. To survive, all wildlife needs food, water, cover, and shelter for raising their young.

Water is as important for birds as food. They need fresh water every day especially during the summer weather. Always place a birdbath close to a shrub or tree to offer a bird an escape route when its feathers are wet and it can only fly a few feet. Most birds prefer water in a birdbath to be no more than two inches deep.

Birds are smart and unpredictable especially when it comes to bird feeders. It is amazing how quickly they can find a new feeder when you put it up. Birds have to see seeds and feeders. They cannot smell, so it may take them several weeks to find some feeders. Since all birds do not require the same type of food, a variety of seeds in different types of feeders such as squirrel-proof, tube, and wooden will attract a mixture of species.

Many birds are seed eaters and those that can crack seeds get more energy from black oil sunflower seeds. Safflower seeds are among the most popular menu item with finches, chickadees, titmice, jays, cardinals, nuthatches, and grosbeaks. Grackles and squirrels will not eat safflower seeds. To get a variety of birds at your feeders, put a mixture of seeds in your feeders.

Some birds such as slate-colored juncos, brown thrashers, rufous-sided towhees, and sparrows are ground feeders, so throw some seeds on the ground for them, especially in cold weather.

Mockingbirds, robins, bluebirds, and cedar waxwings enjoy eating fruit and berries. Beside having bird feeders in your yard, you must have natural vegetation that provides berries, seeds, and nectar to attract these birds.

He who plants a garden plants happiness.
— Chinese Proverb

ℋummingbird Feeding Facts

- Hummingbirds in the United States feed on flower nectar and many small insects. Your garden should provide a healthy, steady diet of both.

- Hummingbird feeders should be hung in the shade, and cleaned and refilled every two to three days under normal circumstances. Use a solution of one part table sugar to four parts water brought to a boil and then cooled and stored in the refrigerator for future use. You do not need to add red coloring. Do not use honey.

- Spread your hummingbird foods–flowers and feeders–throughout your entire garden to discourage dominance by any one bird. Hummingbird friendly flowers, unlike flowers for butterflies, are attractive to these birds whether in the sun or shade.

- Hummingbirds usually return in late March, they usually leave in October – November. Hang your feeders accordingly.

- Pesticides, especially sprays, can be lethal to hummers. Even if they do not take in enough nectar dosed with Malathion, Sevin or Diazinon to kill then directly, the number of small insects available to them in your garden will drop precipitously. This may cause starvation and/or death of the young.

- **Plants that most successfully attract hummingbirds:**
  trumpet honeysuckle, bee-balm, trumpet-creeper, cardinal-flower, scarlet petunia, cypress vine, coral bells, scarlet salvia

THE MOST FREQUENTLY SEEN BIRDS IN S.C. BACKYARDS

Year-round Residents

Red-winged Blackbird
Rufous-sided Towhee
Brewer's Blackbird
Downy Woodpecker
Eastern Bluebird
Hairy Woodpecker
Northern Cardinal
Pilated Woodpecker
Carolina Chickadee
Red-bellied Woodpecker
Mourning Dove

Red-headed Woodpecker
House Finch
Carolina Wren
Common Grackle
Brown Thrasher
Blue Jay
Northern Mockingbird
Brown-headed Nuthatch
House Sparrow
White-throated Sparrow
Tufted Titmouse

THE MOST FREQUENTLY SEEN BIRDS IN S.C. BACKYARDS

Migratory Birds

Indigo Bunting
Purple Finch
American Goldfinch
Rose-breasted Grosbeak
Ruby-throated Hummingbird

Slate-colored Junco
Purple Martin
American Robin
Chimney Swift
Cedar Waxwing

Freezing birdseed before filling feeder will deter the seed from sprouting in your flower bed.

Problems with Deer

Sorry, but, discouraging is the best that can be done to combat hungry deer. Try a buffer of the more deer-resistant plants to protect your favorite plants. Some of the following tips sound far out, but if you are desperate, they may be worth a try:

Tips:
- Plants with thorns or fuzzy foliage, strong aromas or toxicity are disliked by deer.
- Deer do not eat or even like to be around ornamental grasses.
- Deer repellent sprays are most effective on woody plants. Ropel gets pretty good reviews. The problem with spraying is that it washes off during rain. Then you must repeat the spray which is both expensive and tedious.
- Fences at least eight feet high.
- Tie soap bars—the smellier the better—in mesh bags, to shrubs or stakes.
- Slightly aged horse manure (or bone meal) spread in problem areas.
- The best deterrent is a big dog.

PLANTS DEER LOVE
Avoid them unless they are very well protected:

Aucuba	Fatsia	Lobelia
Asiatic Lilies	Fruit Trees	Pansies
Azaleas	Hibiscus	Phlox
Camellia	Hosta	Roses
Crocus	Hydrangea	Rudbeckias
Daylilies	Indian Hawthorn	Sedum
(Especially flowers)	Ivy	Tulips

Everyone has enough to do in weeding his own garden.

— Flemish

PLANTS THAT MAY REPEL DEER

Achilliea	Garlic	Thyme
Alium	Mint	Petunia
Nepeta	Salvia	

PLANTS DEER USUALLY DO NOT LIKE

Annuals:
Begonia
Canna
Coleus
Larkspar
Cosmos
Datura
Fuschias
Heliotrope
Morning Glory
Sweet Alyssum
Stock
Poppies
Scented Geraniums
Pentas
Dusty Miller
Marigolds
Verbena
Zinnia

Perennials:
Ferns
Yarrow
Columbine
Trumpet Vine
Plumbago
Shasta Daisy
Clematis
Coreopsis
Foxglove
Lenton Rose
Lantana
Lavender
Ornamental grasses
Russian Sage

Shrubs:
White Forsythia
Barberry
Flowering Quince
Oleander

Spiraea
Leatherleaf Viburnum
Boxwood
Japanese Plum Yew
Daphne
Gardenia
Holly
Juniper
Privet

Trees:
Red Maple
River Birch
Deodora Cedar
Dogwood
Leyland Cypress
Gingko
Crape Myrtle
Southern Magnolia
Spruce
Scots (& White) Pine
Cherry Laurel

If we walk in the woods, we must feed the mosquitoes.
— Ralph Waldo Emerson

Show Your S.C. Pride With a Carolina Fence

The Carolina Fence incorporates symbols of our state. The fence can function as a valuable habitat element while showcasing symbols of natural and cultural history. Most importantly, as a habitat device, the fence has the ability to attract and support native wildlife. Components are as follows.

The split rail fence represents a commonly used fencing style by South Carolinians in the late 1800's and early 1900's as farmers and landowners responded to new laws that required fencing-in livestock. It can be laid out in "snake fashion" with no vertical posts, or as a post and rail fence.

Yellow jessamine can easily be trained across the split rail fence to form a dense and attractive year-round foliage cover. This species is an easily cultivated perennial vine that does best in sunny locations. The yellow jessamine, an evergreen vine indigenous throughout South Carolina, has been celebrated for its showy yellow flowers in March that herald the coming spring. In addition, the fragrant flowers are a first annual source of nectar to many of our desirable native insects such as butterflies and bees as they stir from their overwintering sites.

Blue Granite, the official stone of South Carolina, adds another aesthetic and official state symbol to your Carolina Fence. Add a stone to your arrangement and if it has an indentation to hold water, it can be a bird bath. Plus, butterflies will love to bask in the sun on it!

You can bury a lot of trouble digging in the dirt.

A Carolina wren house, mounted on the fence or on a post nearby, creates a home for our state bird. Wrens are one of our most common backyard visitors and readily adapt to man-made nest boxes. They are also very comfortable being in close proximity to humans. Their activities are a joy to watch and their song is a very pleasant backyard tune. Note that Carolina wrens have a larger body size and require a larger entrance hole, so if you want them to nest in your bird house make sure to select the Carolina style. You can build your own wren house or buy one from the S.C. Wildlife Federation.

Native Wildflowers in a mulched planting-bed around your fence can be very attractive to the official state butterfly, the tiger swallowtail. The Garden Club of South Carolina has identified this butterfly species to be of particular interest to South Carolinians because it serves as a pollinator in orchards and gardens.

To turn your Carolina Fence into a complete wildlife habitat, you will need to have a source of water. This can be as simple as adding a bird bath. Remember to clean it regularly.

For more information:
The South Carolina Wildlife Federation
2711 Middleburg Drive, Suite 104
Columbia, South Carolina 29204
(803)256-0670 fax (803)256-0690
e-mail: mail@scfw.org
web site: www.scwf.org

Let your prayers for a good crop be short - and your hoeing be long.
— Albanian

Application for Certification

Take heart, you needn't be a zoologist or botanist to fill out this application. The National Wildlife Federation and its Affiliate Organization in your state look forward to acknowledging your efforts in providing habitat for wildlife where you live or work. Do your best to fill out this application, and if there are problems, we'll get back to you with some suggestions. Within 6-8 weeks of receiving your application, we'll forward to you a beautiful personalized certificate suitable for framing and you have the option of purchasing a yard sign to educate others about your project.

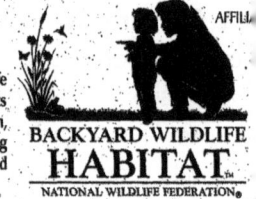

BACKYARD WILDLIFE HABITAT™
NATIONAL WILDLIFE FEDERATION®

A.

Applicant Name _____
Organization Name (if applicable) _____
Name(s) to Appear on Certificate _____
Address of Habitat _____
City _____ County _____
State/Province _____ Country _____ Zip/Postal Code _____
Telephone _____ E-mail Address _____
Property Size (Sq. Ft. or Acres) _____

Office Use:
Habitat # _____
Fee Rcvd. _____
Certified _____
C.S. _____
Key Words _____

B.
If you are applying for someone else, or for an organization, in addition to the above, please fill out the following:

Contact Name _____
Address _____
City _____ State/Province _____
Country _____ Zip/Postal Code _____
Telephone _____ E-mail Address _____
To which address should correspondence be sent? ☐ A ☐ B
Have you ever applied for certification before? ☐ Yes ☐ No If yes, list Habitat # _____

1. FOOD/Plantings and Feeders

A. Do your best to list those plants on your property that might provide wildlife foods such as acorns, berries, nuts, seeds, buds, or nectar.

Large Trees	No.	Small Trees	No.	Shrubs	No.	Annuals & Perennials	N

B. List the type and number of feeders and foods that you provide for wildlife.

Feeder Type	No.	Foods	Visited By

2. WATER/Drinking, Bathing

A. We provide water: ☐ Throughout the year ☐ Seasonally
B. We provide water in: ☐ Bird Bath ☐ Water dripping into a bird bath
☐ Spring ☐ Pond
☐ Water Garden ☐ Other (describe):
☐ Stream

3. COVER/Places to Hide

We provide wind-breaks and places for wildlife to hide from predators in the following manner:
☐ Dense Shrubs (which types?) _____
☐ Evergreen Shrubs (which types?) _____
☐ Brush Piles ☐ Log Piles ☐ Rock Piles/Walls ☐ Ground Covers ☐ Meadow, Scrub, or Prairie Patch
☐ Other (describe): _____

4. PLACES TO RAISE YOUNG

We provide the following for nesting birds, denning mammals, egg-laying reptiles and amphibians, fish, butterflies, and other insects and invertebrates.
☐ Mature Trees (which types?) _____
☐ Small Trees (which types?) _____
☐ Shrub Masses (which types?) _____
☐ Trees with Nest/Den Cavities ☐ Dens in Ground/Rock ☐ Water Garden/Pond ☐ Nesting Boxes
☐ Nesting Shelves ☐ Meadow, Prairie, or Scrub Patch: Size _____ sq. ft.

Which animals use them (birds, squirrels, bats, frogs, dragonflies, etc.)? _____

Plants for butterfly caterpillars (which types?) _____

5. RESOURCE CONSERVATION

We are conserving water and other natural resources in our backyard and community by:
☐ Establishing a backyard wetland or drainage buffer areas ☐ Eliminating chemical use
 to filter storm water and limit runoff ☐ Using a drip soaker hose instead of a sprinkler
☐ Capturing roof rain water for use in planted areas ☐ Controlling pests by organic means or by
☐ Mulching encouraging beneficial insects
☐ Planting native plants suited to the area ☐ Greatly reducing or eliminating lawn areas

---

Please include a rough sketch or landscape diagram of your yard. If you would like to do so, enclose some photographs of your habitat and of you, your family or friends working in and enjoying your habitat. We cannot return the photos or sketch, however, so please be sure you have duplicates for your own use. Kindly keep your submission to a size no larger than could fit in an 11" x 17" envelope. Be sure to keep a copy of your completed application in case we need to contact you about your habitat.

Remember to submit the $15 Program Enrollment Fee (check or money order) to cover our processing and handling costs. Make check payable to the National Wildlife Federation and send to:

Backyard Wildlife Habitat™ Program
National Wildlife Federation
8925 Leesburg Pike
Vienna, VA 22184-0001

Keep in Mind...
• Allow 6-8 weeks for processing of application
• $15 application fee waived if you move and wish to certify your new home
• $5 charge for a second certificate
• Be sure to enclose your payment!

For more information about the Backyard Wildlife Habitat program, visit www.nwf.org on the World Wide Web or contact NWF's Affiliate Organization in your state:

S.C. Wildlife Federation
2711 Middleburg Drive
Suite 104
Columbia, S.C. 29204
(803) 256-0670

"Kinder" Gardening
Fun and educational plants for children.

- **Grow gourds.** They can be made into birdhouses, bath sponges, spoons or even magical creatures.

- **Grow popcorn.** Especially the strawberry variety which grows to kids height and has red ears resembling jumbo strawberries.

- **Grow sunflowers.** They are easy to grow and amazing at 10 feet tall. Remember to gather the seeds for snacks for the kids and the birds.

- **Grow fun plants** that open and close with the sun like morning glories, four o'clocks, and moonflower vine.

- **Grow easy food** like radishes, beans (asparagus beans can grow to 36 inches!) and berries (blueberries, blackberries, raspberries, strawberries). See edible plants in this book, but also talk about poisonous plants.

- **Grow pumpkins,** and use a pen to scratch your childs name on the skin. It will scab over, and the name will grow with the pumpkin!

June brings tulips, lilies, roses,
Fills the children's hands with posies.

- **Grow easy, colorful flowers** from seeds like zinnias, portulaca, petunias and nasturtiums.

- **Grow, smell and eat herbs.** Remember catnip for the cat!

- **Grow a Bean Tepee.** Pole beans are traditional for this kind of project (scarlet runner is best), but you can use morning-glories or climbing nasturtiums. Set three or four poles in the ground to form a tepee, and tie them securely at the top. When the vines appear, guide them onto the strings and poles and soon the tent will be covered. You will be amazed at the heavy yield of pole beans.

- **Grow free houseplants from the grocery store.** Many plants can be raised from avocado and date pits, orange, grapefruit, and lemon seeds, carrot tops, and sweet potatoes.

- **Grow a Pineapple Plant.** First cut the crown (top growth) with a sharp knife, leaving a small amount of the pulpy fruit attached. Pull enough leaves from the base of the crown so that an inch of the "stem" is visible. Next, place about 1 inch of gravel in the bottom of a 4 or 5 inch pot. Fill the pot 3/4 full with porous potting mix. Third, put the crown into the center of the pot and add enough mix to fill within an inch of the pot. Sprinkle about 1/2 inch of sand over the top of the pot, press gently around the crown and water throughly. Allow 3 to 4 weeks for the roots of your new bromeliad to form in the sand and find their way into the richer soil. Give it indirect light. Once established, the pineapple will need direct sunlight at least four hours a day and mild temperatures. Water approximately weekly, allowing the soil to dry out between waterings. Fertilize like houseplants.

A good garden may have some weeds.
— Proverb

Water Gardening

Tips:
- Build a pond where you can enjoy it from the house.
- A pond should be at least two feet deep. Not many gardeners want a smaller pond but most wish they had gone larger. Smaller ponds can be harder to regulate. Try and go no smaller than 8 by 11 feet.
- Strive for a balanced ecosystem to avoid a lot of chemicals.
- A pump is the heart of the pond system. Do your research.
- Do not build a pond in the lowest point of your garden, because problems can occur from runoff.
- Locate water features away from deciduous trees with a lot of debris.
- Consider a waterfall. It will provide wonderful sounds and can be a beautiful focal point, as well as serve an aeration purpose.
- A layer of rocks and gravel on the bottom will act as a natural biological filter.
- Ponds will always have some algae, but they should not turn pea soup green. If they do it is probably because there is too much nitrogen, which can come from too much waste (plant and/or fish). Regularly skimming the pond of leaves is a necessity.
- Plants can occupy about 40 percent of the water's surface.
- Do include fish like koi, goldfish, perch or even bass. They are beneficial to the ecosystem balance.
- Good plants to include are water lilies, ribbon grass, eel grass, cattails, cannas, and water iris.
- Avoid loosestrife, a very bad invasive plant, especially in natural waters. Never dispose of your plants, like water hyacinth or water lettuce, in natural ponds.
- Remember "ponds" in a bucket are a fun small start.

Good sources for additional information:
North America Water Garden Society; www.nawgs.com
Aquascape Designs; www.aquascapedesigns.com
www.absoluteaquatics.com; Hopkins, SC (803)783-1928

No rain, no rainbows.

Garden & Landscape Design

DESIGN:

The main goals for garden design are usually: comfort, privacy, convenience, safety, esae of maintenance, and flexibility. Remember to look past your own property lines for "borrowed" views. Do plan on ways to accentuate good views and hide unsightly ones.

PREPARE:

- **Site Plan** - Property survey with topographical information, such as high and low areas, kinds of soil, drainage, sun and wind directions. Start with a sketch on grid paper.
- **Growing Conditions** - Soil, sun, water and temperatures.
- **Palette** - Color, size, texture of plant material.
- **Research** - See our book and catalogue lists, talk to local green thumbs, observe what succeeds in your area.
- **Soil** - Get a soil analysis, learn pH, texture, drainage.
- **Irrigation** - Provide necessary systems (a must here).

PLANT:

- Purchase, or better yet, get "passalongs."
- Follow (and keep for reference) cultivation tips for each plant you put in your garden. Start a notebook with plastic sleeves into which you can store the plant labels.

CARE:

This includes: pruning, deadheading, mulching, pinching, thinning, supporting, fertilizing, controlling pests and diseases, irrigation, and weeding.

ENJOY:

- Encourage birds and butterflies.
- Arrange flowers.
- Harvest fruits and vegetables.
- Share your garden and the love of gardening.

A hedge between keeps friendships green.

— Mother Goose

Decorating the Mansion for Christmas

The Columbia Garden Club has been privileged to have been invited for many years to decorate the Governor's Mansion for Christmas. Here are some things to try when decorating your mansion.

BLEACHED PINE CONES

Put cones into the bottom of a large plastic container and cover with bleach. Weight the cones with a piece of scrap wood to keep them from floating. Soak for 12 hours or overnight. The cones will close. Drain and dry the cones. They will be ready to use when they have opened back up in a day or two. Wrap gold thread around the stem ends for hanging. They are also nice to use in a bowl or basket as a table accent.

"FIRE GLO" PINE CONES

These pine cones will create many colors when tossed on the fire. A large basket of these makes a nice gift.

Pine cones to fill container
2 gallons of water
1 pound of copper sulphate, dissolved
1 pound of Rock salt

Make a solution of the ingredients in a large bucket and mix well before adding cones. Submerge the cones in the solution for 3 weeks, weighting with a board. Dry.

PINE GARLAND

Sprigs of Pine, approximately 8 to 9 inches long
Cord or twine to use as a base
Spool of #20 gauge floral wire
Wire Cutters

Hold a bunch of 3-4 sprigs and the cord in left hand and the spool of wire in the right. Wrap the wire around the stems and cord about 4 times. Do not cut the wire. Assemble another bunch of 3 to 4 sprigs and lay them in the same direction on the first bunch several inches from the end so that it overlaps the first bunch and covers the stems. Twist the wire tightly around a few times. Be careful to wrap the stems only; if the needles are wrapped, it will spoil the fullness of the roping. Keep the bunches of sprigs uniform. Continue wiring bunches in the same direction. At the end, attach the last bunch in the opposite direction. Then cut the wire. Holly, boxwood, and white pine make beautiful garlands.

Lyme Disease

Lyme disease is a multi-system disease affecting humans, caused by a spirochete (Borrelia burgdorferi). There are over 100 strains of this bacteria in the United States. Lyme disease is transmitted to humans by the bite of an infected tick, which can be found anywhere in the state. In the South, we are at risk year around. Lyme can mimic numerous diseases (ex: fibromyalgia, multiple sclerosis, Alzheimer's, chronic fatigue syndrome, ALS, lupus, etc.). This makes a correct diagnosis difficult. Treatment is with antibiotics.

Early symptoms may appear days or weeks after an infected tick bite. About 60% of people notice a bull's eye rash, which can vary in size and shape from very small to large. It can be a red ring with central clearing or it can mimic other skin problems such as hives, eczema, poison ivy, flea or spider bites, etc. If a rash appears, photograph it and see your doctor right away! Some patients, but not all, have flu-like symptoms. If untreated, serious complications develop. Later symptoms may occur in any combination, may come and go, vary in intensity, and are different in every patient. General symptoms may be fatigue, headaches, fever, swollen glands, weight change.

RESOURCES:
- Lyme Disease Network of S.C. (803) 798-5963
- Lyme Disease Foundation (860) 525-2000

DIAGNOSIS AND TREATMENT

Lyme disease remains a clinical diagnosis that is primarily based on signs and symptoms. Results of serological testing are supportive, but "no test can definitively rule out Lyme disease." It is treatable with antibiotics, which are usually recommended for a minimum of four to six weeks. Early treatment gives a better outcome. Inadequate treatment will result in relapse and complications. Late diagnosis can result in longer-term treatment, chronic infection, and disability.

PREVENTION

Avoid tick-infested areas like bushes and tall grass. Do not sit directly on the ground. Wear light-colored long pants and long sleeves so ticks can be seen easily. Tuck shirt into pants and pants into socks to protect bare skin. Do frequent tick checks, including a full body check upon returning inside. Use EPA-approved tick repellent. If bitten: Proper tick removal is done with fine-point tweezers placed next to the skin. Do not squeeze the body or try to burn or smother the tick. Pull the tick straight out. Wash hands, disinfect tweezers and the bite site. Save the tick in a small jar with a moist piece of cotton and mark your calendar. Have the tick identified and tested by a lab.

RELIABLE BOOKS

- *Coping With Lyme Disease – A Practical Guide to Diagnosis and Treatment*
  By Denise Lang

- *Everything You Need To Know About Lyme Disease*
  By Karen Vanderhoof-Forschner

HINTS FOR DESIGNING
Flower Arrangements

Arrangements with small potted plants are easy. Replace small pots with plastic bags (sandwich bags) to hold in moisture. Make sure soil is moist but not soggy. May need to tie with a twisty at the base of stem. Great plants for this are small ferns, ivy and whatever is blooming. It is easy to get these plants all year long at the home supply store or even the grocery store. Cover the arrangement's base with moss.

Always make sure your "mechanics" are well covered. Mechanics are the things that hold the arrangement together. Examples include water proof tape, metal frogs, chicken wire (crumple up a 2 inch piece into a ball), and floral foam (oasis). Good things to hide the mechanics are moss or any live part of the arrangement – especially the greenery. If you use Spanish moss from our own Low Country, you must treat it for insects. A quick way is to wrap fresh moss in newspaper and microwave for one minute. (Isn't technology great?!)

Make sure there is some way to hold water for the plants. A tuna-fish can painted black works great in many situations (wicker baskets, open wire baskets). When using oasis, leave room for water. Holes need to touch water, facing down.

Strip leaves off any stems that are submerged in water. Recut stems before placing in oasis.

Many special holders can be bought at a florist supply store. Buy the best clippers you can afford. An apron with big pockets helps keep track of clippers.

Be creative in clear containers when filling the bottom of the container. Try marbles, pebbles, citrus fruit (whole, not cut), cranberries, and decorative foliage. But do remember to have the bottom match the top.

Gardening, just another day at the plant.

Floppy stemmed short plants can be helped by placing the short stem in a larger hollow stem. Floppy stems and short stems should be wrapped with a floral pick, wire, bamboo stick or use a water vial. When adding candles, use a special candle pick.

It is very important to have your arrangement well-secured. Nothing is worse than the arrangement falling into the plate of your guest! Use wire, pin holders, floral foam (oasis), and lots of waterproof tape. Green tape is usually best. If you are using a vertical vase, weigh it down with sand, small pebbles, melted paraffin wax or kitty litter. If it is very top heavy, you may need to put a brick in the bottom.

If the container is too heavy, consider filling the bottom with some lightweight packing peanuts. These also work well in planted containers.

Be careful of thorns on roses, if you will be arranging them a lot (lucky you!) then invest in good "thorn strippers." Strip the bottom 6 inches for ease in arranging.

Change water daily or at least check to see if additional water should be added. A flower additive like " Flora-life" is a good idea. You may experiment with some home additives to the water like Sprite (not diet), Clorox, sugar & lemon juice.

Try to use at least three different kinds of greenery for contrast and interest.

Good flower design can be anything you like. But do remember the basics of good art: form – triangles and domes are good; line – careful for that odd man out; color – think of the color wheel; light – natural vs. artificial, which reflects on to the arrangement; and lightness vs. darkness of the actual arrangement; texture – usually the more the better; size and proportion.

You may need to spritz daily with water ivy, hydrangeas, and gardenias because they take water through their flowers and leaves.

Nature is the art of God.
— Dante

ANNUALS THAT MAKE GOOD CUT FLOWERS

Daisy	Larkspur
Cosmos	Zinnia
Scarlet Sage	Sunflower
Money Plant	Nasturtium
Snapdragon	Bachelor's Button
Poppy	Sweet Pea

GARDEN PLANTS FOR ARRANGING
- **Sasanqua** - flowers do not hold up but foliage is great.
- **Camellia** - flowers and foliage work well.
- **Acuba** - solid and variegated are nice.
- **Pittsporum** - variegated is especially nice.
- **Boxwood** - covers a multitude of sins, but careful, it can be over used.
- **Privet** - careful, it can overtake your garden.
- **Andromeda Pieris** - plant is pretty year round.
- **Cast iron plant** - do fun things with leaf, like roll & twist.
- **Hydrangeas** - blooms into Oct., don't use leaves.
- **Chinese Lanterns** - wonderful but it can be invasive.

PLANTS NOT SO GOOD IN ARRANGEMENTS
(because most will wilt too quickly)
- nandina, lantana, swamp sunflower
  (so tempting because it is blooming in the fall)

WHEN TO CUT:
The cool of the evening is the best time to cut, especially in hot weather, for most plants. This gives them a maximum amount of plant food which has been

---

You buy some flowers for your table: you tend them tenderly as you're able: You fetch them water from hither and thither – What thanks do you get for it all? They wither.

— Samuel Hoffenstein

stored during the day, and preserves them longer. The second best time is early morning. Stems are either woody or soft, and must be handled according to the structure of the plant. Conditioning in the dark is most effective as the many tiny pores on the underside of the leaves are closed at night, and in the dark. This helps to retain moisture.

CUTTING PLANT MATERIAL FROM YOUR GARDEN:
A plastic pail with rolled edges is preferred. These are light to carry and less likely to injure blooms and foliage than a metal bucket. Wind is an enemy to cut flowers. In very breezy weather place pail in a sheltered spot against a building. With a bucket of warm water close at hand, cut material and put immediately into water. Do not crowd material. When inside, spread newspaper on the counter and remove material from the pail, one stem at a time, being careful not to bruise or tear blooms or foliage. As each stem is removed, strip foliage that will be below water level in finished arrangements. Remove thorns from roses. When a flower stem is cut, air seeps into the lower stem and blocks the continuous flow of moisture to the plant. If this can be prevented, the flower will last much longer. For flowers that wilt easily, re-cut stems under water at an angle. Leave in deep water to harden overnight. (Other methods will be listed later)

A GUIDE FOR CUTTING AT PROPER STAGE OF MATURITY:
- **Annuals:** As soon as they are open or two-thirds open. Avoid day-old blooms.
- **Bulbous Flowers:** Half open if possible.
- **Camellia:** Freshly opened.
- **Chrysanthemum:** Freshly opened.
- **Dahlia:** Two-thirds open
- **Day-Lily:** In bud, showing color
- **Fruit trees:** Flowering: In bud, showing color.
- **Gardenia:** In bud, or just opening
- **Iris:** In bud, showing color, half-opened
- **Perennials:** Freshly opened
- **Roses:** To keep in bud, after calyx has turned back and a few petals have unfurled. To use next day, one-quarter to one-half open.
- **Spike Flowers:** (delphinium, larspur, lily-of-the-valley, lupine, snapdragon, stock). Lower floret, freshly opened, upper florets in bud.

You're Probably a Designer if...

Written by Ruth Moorehead of Indiana

- ... You remember the altar arrangement but not the sermon
- ... You read about a carpet sale and go to collet cardboard tubes
- ... Your best souvenirs from Florida are barnacles
- ... Your florist knows more about your taste than your family
- ... Your golf bag has ever held more pine cones than golf balls
- ... The main reason you go to a bar is to collect mini bottles
- ... You have ever considered using a bowling ball as a container
- ... You've ever removed your car's back seat before a flower show
- ... You're fresh out of pantyhose, but have floral tape in every color
- ... You see car parts garbage and think design potential
- ... You've ever point-scored a chef's salad
- ... You've ever used your washing machine for flower conditioning
- ... And finally, you have more pinholders than underwear...

... **You are probably a designer!**

TREATMENTS FOR DIFFICULT FLOWERS:

- **Burning the Stems Method:**
  The stems of plants which exude a milky substance when cut, such as the poinsettia, should be held over an open flame which is as hot as possible in order that the period of burning may be kept to a minimum. The leaves and flowers should be protected by wrapping in damp cloth. A similar effect may be obtained by immersing the stems in boiling water.

- **Boiling Water Treatment:**
  This method is particularly effective for flowers such as roses, chrysanthemums, daisies, liatris, hydrangeas, and dahlias, whose stems are firm on the outside but soft within. Cut the stems then put them in two inches of boiling water for five minutes. The boiling water forces the air in the stems to expand slightly and escape. The submerged parts of the stems may lose color. Put in cold water immediately and the stems become sturdy again. Protect leaves and flowers from steam. Wrap in damp paper or cloth.

- **Chemical Treatment:**
  When using any chemical the general procedure is first to cut the stem while immersed in water, then to dry the stem, and finally to apply the capisum, alcohol and vinegar. The plant should be dipped in the chemical for a few seconds and conditioned.

- **Increasing the Area of Absorption:**
  Flowers and leaves may benefit from misting; however, some flowers may water spot or turn color. Another simple treatment is to scrape the bottom two or three inches or crush the clipped ends of the stem, or split them vertically into four parts with a sharp pair of scissors or a knife, so as to increase the water absorbing area. Cutting the stem on a slant increases the absorption area and facilitates insertion into a needle point. This is the general rule for cutting all plant material.

From the earth we were formed, to the earth we return and in between we garden.

CUTTING THE STEMS UNDER WATER:

This is the most commonly used and most effective of all the techniques. It seals the stem from absorbing air and is generally used for all plants irrespective of other methods which may be applied later. For some plants this method alone is considered adequate.

FLOWERS BEST CUT IN WATER:

agapanthus, anthurium, baby's breath, begonia, bird of paradise, caladium, carnation, cattleya, celosia, coleus (and split ends), cymbidium, daffodil, daylily, delphinium, dianthus, Easter lily, eucalyptus, gladiolus, hosta (and split ends), iris, liatris, ligustrum (and split ends), loquat (and split ends), pampas grass, Periwinkle, petunia (and lightly crush stems), philodendron, phoenix, quince (and split stem), spirea, viburnum (and crush ends)

Salt: Add 1 tablespoon of salt to each quart of water for hardening.

Sugar: Add 1 tablespoon of sugar to each quart of water for hardening.

Submerging: Submerge completely in cold water for a half an hour before regular hardening.

Vinegar and Sugar:
(to acidify alkaline water) Used for acid loving plants like azaleas. Add 1 tablespoon of sugar and 1 tablespoon vinegar to each quart of water for hardening.

Where the sun does not enter, the doctor does.

— Italian Proverb

PARTICULAR PLANTS:
- **Amaryllis:** Cut in water. Wrap cut end with floral tape to prevent curling.
- **Anemone:** Cut in water. When they begin to droop, dip stem ends in alcohol for a few seconds, or apply salt to ends.
- **Asparagus Fern:** Use boiling water method.
- **Aspidistra:** Cut in water. Tie in shape desired.
- **Aster:** Harden 12 hours in a solution of 1 tsp. sugar to 1 quart of water.
- **Autumn Leaves:** Split stems slightly. Stand in solution of 2 parts glycerin to 1 part water. Add water when necessary for 20 days.
- **Bamboo:** After bamboo has been cut it will not draw up water. To overcome this, drill or pierce a hole down through the center of the main branch to the bottom node, then fill each section with water.
- **Banana Plant:** Cut in water, apply lemon juice or vinegar to all cut edges to prevent discoloring.
- **Bells of Ireland:** Cut in water. Harden overnight.
- **Black Eyed Susan:** Cut in water. If they begin to droop, re-cut end and use boiling water method.
- **Bougainvillea:** Split woody stems. Strip unnecessary foliage.
- **Caladium:** Rub salt into the cut ends.
- **Calla Lilly:** Cut in water. Rub stem ends with salt. Let stand for a few minutes then re-cut in fresh water.
- **Camellia:** Cut in water. Press dressmaker's pin through center of blossom into stem to hold it firmly in place, or shake a little salt into each blossom.

- **Canna Lilly:** Cut in water. Inject water into the leaves by means of a pump.

- **Chrysanthemum:** Cut in water. Scrape, or crush stem ends, or break stems with fingers. For wilting plants, break stems with fingers and use boiling water method, then stand in cold water overnight.

- **Dahlia:** Dip in boiling water for a few seconds or crush the cut ends slightly and dip in alcohol for a few seconds.

- **Dogwood:** Split stem ends and stand in warm water overnight.

- **Dusty Miller:** Char stems and harden for 1-1 1/2 days in water.

- **Elaeagnus:** Burn cut ends then quickly dip in alcohol.

- **Evergreens & Pines:** Split stems and stand in deep cold water overnight. Spray lightly from below with clear lacquer.

- **Ferns:** Put in water overnight or lay flat wrapped in damp newspaper.

- **Gardenia:** Dip in alcohol for a few seconds.

- **Geraniums:** Use boiling water method.

- **Gerber Daisy:** Use boiling water method.

- **Grasses and Reeds:** Dip stem ends in vinegar for three minutes. Stand in solution of 1 pint vinegar to 3 parts water for at least 10-12 minutes.

- **Holly:** Split stem ends and condition in water overnight.

- **Hydrangea:** Use boiling water or burning method.

- **Ivy:** Cut through a node. Wash foliage in lukewarm water. Submerge completely in cold water for 3 hours. Set in 3" of water overnight. Add a piece of charcoal to water.

- **Ligustrum:** Split stem ends. Condition in water.

- **Loquat:** Split stem ends. Condition in water.

- **Magnolia:** Split stem ends or use burning method.

- **Maidenhair Fern:** char stem ends. Lay flat in newspaper and submerge in cold water overnight

- **Marigold:** Cut in water. When leaves start to droop, use boiling water method.

- **Nandina:** char stem end. Soak completely in water for 30 minutes. Stand in 5" water overnight. Add a pinch of salt to vase of water.
- **Periwinkle:** Cut in water. Use boiling water method.
- **Petunia:** Cut in water. Crush stem ends lightly.
- **Poinsettia:** Cut in water then use boiling water or burning method.
- **Quince:** Split stem ends underwater.
- **Roses:** Cut in water then crush stem ends or use boiling water method. Add sugar.
- **Snapdragons:** Cut in water or use boiling water.
- **Spirea:** Split stem ends.
- **Stock:** Crush the cut ends.
- **Sunflower:** Dip in vinegar for a few seconds.
- **Tulip:** Cut in water. To prevent stems from dropping, open blooms and insert wire down through stems. Then close and pinch stems very gently just under the blooms.
- **Verbina:** Cut in water and crush stem ends.
- **Viburnum:** Cut in water and crush stem ends.
- **Wisteria:** (in flower) Split stem ends and peel back bottom inch of bark, then crush. Stand in alcohol. Use burning method for large branches or foliage.
- **Zinnia:** Cut in water. Remove unnecessary foliage. If leaves begin to wilt, use boiling water method.
- **Cattails:** Spray cattails with hairspray, to avoid a blow out.

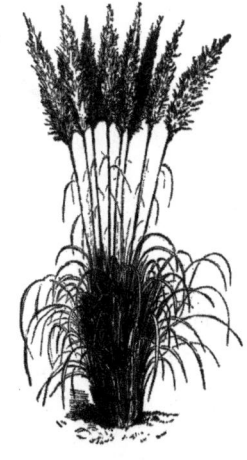

Fire Ant Management

In South Carolina, fire ants are found in many lawns and gardens. Their mounds are not only unsightly, but gardeners can also quickly receive multiple stings before realizing they have disturbed a nest. Fire ants are generally active in South Carolina between the months of March and mid November.

Fire ants build their home both above and below the ground. After mating, the queen burrows into the ground to lay her eggs. Worker ants then expand the nest both below and above the ground. The reason for this is to create a positive airflow and thus regulate moisture and temperature.

The key to eradication of a fire ant nest is to kill the queen which is not an easy task. Ants feed by a process known as trophallaxis, meaning one ant feeds another. Solid food is predigested to convert it to a liquid, and passed on to the queen and the others. Therefore, ant bait must act slowly in order to reach the queen. Quicker acting bait kills the food carrier before it feeds the queen.

There are many useful products available for fire ant control, and most of them are quite effective when properly applied. However, ants reproduce so quickly that control may be short term. Although ants are territorial, they are invasive with no natural enemies other than each other. Baiting all mounds may destroy those mounds but still miss those ants whose mound has not yet become apparent. In other instances, ants in neighboring yards and adjacent fields move readily and easily into your recently cleared or treated property.

What a man needs in gardening is a cast-iron back with a hinge on it.

— Charles Dudleywarner

The Clemson University Department of Horticulture recommends the Two-Step Method of Fire Ant Control for use twice each year. The first step is to broadcast the bait insecticide over the entire yard using the smallest opening available on your spreader. Commercially available baits include Amdro, Award (formally Logic), and PT 370 and may be applied anytime during the warm season, but it is most effective when the ants are foraging for food. This can be determined by placing bait on a small piece of white paper adjacent to an active mound. If ants are seen taking the bait within 30 minutes, it is a good time to treat the whole area. Ants are most active when soil temperature is at least 70 degrees and less than 95 degrees. In summer ants are most active in late afternoon and early evening. Using fresh bait ensures maximum efficiency of the product. Use within two years and store in a tightly sealed container.

Step two calls for baiting treatments of individual mounds no sooner than seven days after step one. This treatment should be confined to those mounds adjacent to high traffic areas and those along building foundations. Environmental concerns suggest that bait treatment, though slower acting, will generally eliminate the problem with the least effort without leaving a surface residue.

*D*ID YOU KNOW?

- *Insects are the most successful life form on Earth!*
- *Ladybugs help control mealy bugs.*
- *Many moths use the moon to navigate at night. Street lights confuse moths and that's why they end up circling the light.*

I have a rock garden.
Last week three of them died.

— Richard Diran

Great Reference Books... Great Reading

Armitage, Allan M.
Armitage's Garden Annuals;
Armitage's Garden Perennials

Bender and Rushing
Passalong Plants – Entertaining and informative about easy southern plants.

Chaplin, Lois Trigg
The Southern Gardener's Book of Lists

Dirr, Michael
Manual of Woody Landscape Plants – The American reference to landscape-worthy trees, shrubs, vines – evergreen and deciduous.
Trees and Scrubs for Warm Climates

DiSabato-Augt, Tracy
The Well-Tended Perennial

Eyewitness Garden Books
Pruning and Training

Grant, Greg and William C. Welch
The Southern Heirloom Garden

Halfacre and Shaw
Landscape Plants of the Southeast – A good beginner's book; great for trees and shrubs.

Harper, Pamela
Designing with Perennials – Principles of garden design and plant combinations, from Virginia. Excellent reference, excellent reading.

Hill and Braclay
Southern Herb Growing

Horton, Orene
: *Clippings from Orene's Garden*

Lawrence, Elizabeth, Edited by Nancy Goodwin
: *A Southern Garden* – Personal stories...a joy to read. She has many good books.

Mitchell, Henry...has many funny personal stories.

Ogden
: *Garden Bulbs for the South* – Lots of information on heritage bulbs.

Polomski, Bob
: *Month by Month Gardening in the Carolinas*

The Southern Living Garden Book

Rochester, Margot
: *Earthly Delights*

Tripp and Raulston
: *The Year in Trees* – For the southeast. Raulston has many fine books.

Trustees' Garden Club of Savannah, Georgia
: *Garden Guide for the Lower South*

Welch, William
: *Perennial Garden Color*
: *Antique Roses for the South* – Excellent reference.

Wilson, Jim
: *Bulletproof Flowers for the South*

Must have: *The South Carolina Midlands Master Gardener Annual Calender.* This is especially good for month by month tasks as well as what plants are blooming. It has a lot of information for vegetable & flower gardeners.

If you have a garden and a library, you have everything you need.
— Cicero

EVERYTHING YOU EVER WANTED TO KNOW,
...Answers by a Smart Neighbor

- **Clemson Extension Service, Home & Garden Information**
  Phone 1-888-656-9988
  Website .... www.hgic.clemson.edu
  They have many good pamphlets.

- **Richland County Extension Service**
  Phone .... (803) 865-1216
  900 Clemson Road, Sandhill Research Center
  Columbia, SC 29224

- **Lexington County Extension Service**
  Phone .... (803) 359-8515
  605 West Main Street
  Lexington, S.C. 29072

- **Magazines:**
  Carolina Gardner
  Southern Living

  > **ON THE WEB:**
  > Handbook of South Carolina Gardens
  > Garden & Landscape Design

- **Television:**
  Making it Grow on SCETV, hosted by Rowland Alston.
  Sumter County Extension Service
  Post Office Box 2377
  Sumter, South Carolina 29151
  Website .... www.mig.org
  Very entertaining, usually airs at least once a week.

Let us be grateful to people who make us happy: they are the charming gardeners who make our souls blossom.

— Marcel Proust

Plant Catalogues are great not only for shopping but, as wonderful sources of information. Don't just throw them away, keep a years supply with your gardening books for reference. File them by seasons – i.e. keep all the spring catalogues together. Barbra J. Barton has written Gardening by Mail; it lists all the catalogues and is certainly worth the trip to the library.

SOME FAVORITE CATALOGUE COMPANIES:

Goodness Grows, Lexington, GA..(706) 743-5055

Park Seed, Greenwood, SC..(800) 845-3369
www.parkseed.com

Plant Delights Nursery...(919) 772-4794
www.plantdelights.com

Singing Springs Nursery...(919) 732-9403
www.singingspringsnursery.com

Wayside Gardens, Hodges, SC..(800) 845-1124
www.waysidegardens.com

White Flower Farm, Litchfield, CT...................................(800) 503-9624

Woodlanders, Aiken, SC...(803) 648-7522
www.woodlanders.net

Wilkerson Mill, Southwest of Atlanta, GA........................(770) 463-2400
www.hydrangea.com

Still – in a way – nobody sees a flower – really – it is so small – we haven't time – and to see takes time, like to have a friend takes time.

— Georgia O'Keeffe

Columbia Gardens to Visit

Riverbanks Botanical Garden ....(803) 779-8717

Woodrow Wilson Boyhood Home ....(803) 252-1770
The Columbia Garden Club has been sponsoring, with funds and member labor, the reconstruction of the gardens. We invite you to visit at 1705 Hampton Street, Columbia, SC.

U.S.C. Horseshoe
The Rose Garden at the Presidents House is a memorial to the Columbia Garden Club's deceased members.

Governor's Mansion Complex
The Mansion, The Lace House and The Boyston House

The State House grounds

OTHER FABULOUS GARDENS AROUND THE STATE:

Brookgreen Gardens, Murrells Inlet, SC ....(843) 237-4218

Cypress Gardens, Moncks Corner, SC..............................(843) 553-0515

Edisto Memorial Garden, Orangeburg, SC

Kalmia Gardens of Coker College, Hartsville, SC

Magnolia Plantation & Its Gardens, Charleston, SC ....(843) 571-1266

Middleton Place, Charleston, SC ....(843) 556-6020

Swan Lake Iris Garden, Sumter, SC

The South Carolina Botanical Garden, Clemson, SC........(864) 656-3405

Notes

www.ingramcontent.com/pod-product-compliance
Lightning Source LLC
Chambersburg PA
CBHW050527170426
43201CB00013B/2119